FREE TO GIVE

FREE TO GIVE

Should Christians Tithe?

BART PETERS

TATE PUBLISHING
AND ENTERPRISES, LLC

Published by Tate Publishing & Enterprises, LLC
127 E. Trade Center Terrace | Mustang, Oklahoma 73064 USA
1.888.361.9473 | www.tatepublishing.com

Tate Publishing is committed to excellence in the publishing industry. The company reflects the philosophy established by the founders, based on Psalm 68:11,
"The Lord gave the word and great was the company of those who published it."

Book design copyright © 2015 by Tate Publishing, LLC. All rights reserved.
Cover design by Niño Carlo Suico
Interior design by Mary Jean Archival

Published in the United States of America

ISBN: 978-1-68164-391-5
Religion / Christian Church / Canon & Ecclesiastical Law
15.09.21

Contents

Author's Note i

Introduction.. 1

1 Every Instance of *Tithe* in the Bible............................. 9

2 What the Tithe Was 19

3 The Law 41

4 Abraham, Melchizedek, and Jesus.................................. 53

5 Before the Law 63

6 Malachi 3 75

7 Did Jesus Endorse the Tithe? 85

8 Jesus on Giving... 99

9 Paul on Giving.. 113

10 The Paradox of the Two Principles of Christian

     Giving 127

11 Freedom... 139

Conclusion.. 151

Author's Note

There is hardly a page of this book that does not have a quote from the Bible on it. So please, have your favorite Bible handy when you read this. There are several places where I suggest that you should put down this book and read a passage in the Bible before continuing. Please do this; it will really help you understand some of the arguments presented. I have also included an index that tells you where to find all of the scripture quotes in *Free to Give*. All Bible quotes come from the New International Version of the Bible, except where otherwise noted. Generally, I do not question the fidelity of the English text to the original. I have found the NIV to be, by far, the most helpful translation in studying this topic as well as others. First, the accompanying study materials to the NIV are second to none, which were a great help to me. Second, in studying and using various translations over the years, I have found that the NIV is the most honest translation.

Because of the number of verses quoted in this book, 278 to be exact, it was necessary to seek permission from the publisher of the NIV to use it in this book. The International Bible Society was very gracious to provide explicit permission in writing to use the NIV so prolifically throughout this book. With all of my caveats out of the way, let me say that I have been tremendously blessed in the research and writing of this book, and I hope that, in like manner, it blesses you too.

Introduction

Why the Issue of Giving Is So Important

For where your treasure is, there your heart will be also.

—Matthew 6:21

I ONCE HEARD a pastor say that giving is where "the rubber meets the road" in our walk with God. Another pastor said that the area of giving is the "acid test" of our faith.

What are these pastors saying?

The issue of giving is not on the periphery of the Christian faith: it is a central and defining issue. I believe that what these pastors are saying is that many of the major principles of Christianity (things like stewardship, integrity, and obedience) are demonstrated by conscious acts of will in the natural world. In particular, I believe they are saying that a Christian's beliefs are manifested in the act of giving. We find similar reasoning in the book of James.

> What good is it my brothers, if a man claims to have faith but has no deeds? Can such a faith save him? Suppose a brother or sister is without clothes and daily food. If one of you says to him, "Go, I wish you well; keep warm and well fed," but does nothing about his physical needs, what good is it? In the same way, faith by itself, if it is not accompanied by action, is dead.
>
> But someone will say, "You have faith; I have deeds."
>
> Show me your faith without deeds, and I will show you my faith by what I do. You believe that there is one God. Good! Even the demons believe that and shudder. (James 2:14–19)

Giving is how your faith, hope, and love find their expression in human terms. If you are a true believer in the Gospel of Jesus Christ, it is only natural that you desire that it would go forth to benefit other people in the way it has benefited you. The founding fathers of America proved how serious they were about independence by financing the American Revolutionary War. In the final sentence of the document that established America as a sovereign nation, it says,

And for the support of this declaration, with a firm Reliance on the Protection of divine Providence, we mutually pledge to each other our lives, our Fortunes, and our sacred Honor. (From the *Declaration of Independence*, July 4, 1776)

American Christians are heirs of the men who gave not only their fortunes but their very lives for the sake of our political freedom. Likewise, I believe the point these pastors are trying to make is that we should be all the more willing to give on behalf of the person that secured for us our spiritual freedom. It is a principle that transcends religion: if you care about something, then you support it. In essence, you *prove* how much you care about something in how you support it.

Jesus himself said, "For where your treasure is, there your heart will be also" (Matt. 6:21).

Notice that Jesus did not say, "For where your heart is, there your treasure will be also."

From a practical standpoint, the second statement seems more accurate. Obviously, just because you give money to a particular cause does not mean you believe in it. Giving does not necessarily affect the heart; your heart affects giving. Jesus repeatedly summoned people to change their hearts, and then what they did in tribute to God would be credited to them. So why did Jesus make this statement the way he did? I believe he was speaking from our perspective. We cannot judge the motives of another person. We only know what we see. And what we can see is how a person stores his treasure or spends his money. Elsewhere in Matthew, Jesus said, "a tree is recognized by its fruit" (Matt. 12:33).

As far as this verse pertains to money, I believe that Jesus was saying that we can recognize the state of a man's heart ("a tree") by how he spends his money ("its fruit").

Therefore, I could not agree more with the statements of the two pastors. Giving is where the talk becomes the walk. Giving is how the ideological and philosophical truths of Christianity become real. And because the matter of Christian giving is so important, I decided to write this book. I feel that the church in America today is largely ignorant of what the Bible really has to say about giving. The predominant teaching on monetary giving in Christianity today (tithing) is not based in truth. In fact, you will see in this book that the modern doctrine of the tithe is not a Christian concept at all, on several levels. Over half of this book is dedicated to tearing down the tithe. In my opinion, the Christian Church must abandon the tithe.

The question is not, "Is it right to give?" Of course it is. I hope no one has the impression that my goal is to divert support away from the local church. But I believe that the manner in which you give is even more important than the amount you give. This is why the modern-day tithe must be confronted. I hope to make it clear that we are not required to give according to old covenant law. Moreover, I believe that Christian giving should not be based on the practices of the Old Testament. Instead, we should act according to the teachings and examples of the New Testament. So the real purpose of this book is to show the reader a new way to give.

> The central message of this book is that we are *free to give* in the way of the Spirit in accordance with the new covenant.

Some may be thinking, "What's the big deal? My church calls the weekly giving a 'tithe,' but it's more of a guideline than a commandment. Why tear down something that seems to be working for the good of the church?"

These are valid questions, and here is my answer: In the beginning of the Christian Church, there was no problem with giving. Read and consider these amazing accounts from the book of Acts.

> They devoted themselves to the apostles' teaching and to the fellowship, to the breaking of bread and to prayer. Everyone was filled with awe, and many wonders and miraculous signs were done by the apostles. All the believers were together and had everything in common. Selling their possessions and goods, they gave to everyone as he had need. (Acts 2:42–45)

> All the believers were one in heart and mind. No one claimed that any of his possessions was his own, but they shared everything they had. With great power

the apostles continued to testify to the resurrection of the Lord Jesus, and much grace was upon them all. There were no needy persons among them. For from time to time those who owned lands or houses sold them, brought the money from the sales and put it at the apostles' feet, and it was distributed to anyone as he had need. (Acts 4:32–35)

The big question to me is, "Would the modern Christian Church have ever established the doctrine of the tithe if all Christians throughout history had given in the manner recorded in the book of Acts?"

Is it really true that Christians owe a tithe of their income to their local church? Or is this a doctrine that was contrived in response to the reluctance of modern Christians to give?

We free ourselves to operate in the full measure of the Spirit as we embrace Truth. So it is important that we know the truth about everything in Scripture, not the least of which is how God wants us to give and the role of the tithe in Christian giving. If a church's position on the tithe is that it is a "guideline", then that particular organization, as you will see, is making up its own system of giving and has abandoned what is plainly written in Scripture. In addition, by borrowing terms from the Old Testament and modifying the ideas behind them, a church discounts the wealth of instruction on giving contained in the New Testament (as if there was so little information in the New Testament that we *needed* to adopt ideas from the Old Testament).

Ultimately, *the doctrine and practice of Christian giving must be based in truth.* So the big deal is this: a falsehood is being propagated among the church in America in the area of giving. I believe that what the church sows in untruth, it will reap in spiritual decay. I believe this practice, the tithe, is a spiritual shackle that is holding the church back from its true power to change the world. It is time for the church to wake up and return to true biblical giving. The integrity of our faith and our witness to the world depends on the church returning to true giving.

1

Every Instance of *Tithe* in the Bible

> You are in error because you do not
> know the Scriptures…
>
> —Matthew 22:29

BEFORE YOU READ a single word of analysis, I first present to you every instance in the NIV Bible of the word *tithe* and any of its variants. It is in the interest of integrity that I believe I must start the book this way. This is how it all started for me, and I believe Scripture speaks volumes for itself.

The thirty-one instances of *tithe* and *tithes* in the NIV Bible:

Leviticus 27:30–32

A **tithe** of everything from the land, whether grain from the soil or fruit from the trees, belongs to the Lord. If a man redeems any of his **tithe**, he must add a fifth of the value to it. The entire **tithe** of the herd and flock—every tenth animal that passes under the shepherd's rod—will be holy to the Lord.

Numbers 18:21–28

"I give to the Levites all the **tithes** in Israel as their inheritance in return for the work they do while serving in the Tent of Meeting. From now on the Israelites must not go near the Tent of Meeting, or they will bear the consequences of their sin and die. It is the Levites who are to do the work at the Tent of Meeting and bear the responsibility for offenses against it. This is a lasting ordinance for the generations to come. They will receive no inheritance among the Israelites. Instead, I give to the Levites as their inheritance the **tithes** that the Israelites present as an offering to the Lord. That is why I said concerning them: 'They will have no inheritance among the Israelites.'"

The Lord said to Moses, "Speak to the Levites and say to them: 'When you receive from the Israelites the **tithe** I give you as your inheritance, you must present a tenth of that **tithe** as the Lord's offering. Your offering will be reckoned to you as grain from the threshing floor or juice from the winepress. In this way you also will present an offering to the Lord from all the **tithes** you receive from the Israelites. From these **tithes** you must give the Lord's portion to Aaron the priest.'"

Deuteronomy 12:4–19

You must not worship the Lord your God in their way. But you are to seek the place the Lord your God will choose from among all your tribes to put his Name there for his dwelling. To that place you must go; there bring your burnt offerings and sacrifices, your **tithes** and special gifts, what you have vowed to give and your freewill offerings, and the firstborn of your herds and flocks. There, in the presence of the Lord your God, you and your families shall eat and shall rejoice in everything you have put your hand to, because the Lord your God has blessed you.

You are not to do as we do here today, everyone as he sees fit, since you have not yet reached the resting place and the inheritance the Lord your God is giving you. But you will cross the Jordan and settle in the land the Lord your God is giving you as an inheritance, and he will give you rest from all your enemies around you so that you will live in safety. Then to the place the Lord your God will choose as a dwelling for his Name-there you are to bring everything I command you: your burnt offerings and sacrifices, your **tithes** and special gifts, and all the choice possessions you have vowed to the Lord. And there rejoice before the Lord your God, you, your sons and daughters, your menservants and maidservants, and the Levites from your towns, who have no allotment or inheritance of their own. Be careful not to sacrifice your burnt offerings anywhere you please. Offer them only at the place the Lord will choose in one of your tribes, and there observe everything I command you.

Nevertheless, you may slaughter your animals in any of your towns and eat as much of the meat as you want, as if it were gazelle or deer, according to the blessing the Lord your God gives you. Both the ceremonially unclean and the clean may eat it. But you must not eat the blood; pour it out on the ground like water. You must not eat in your own towns the **tithe** of your grain and new wine and oil, or the firstborn of your herds and flocks, or whatever you have vowed to give, or your freewill offerings or special gifts. Instead, you are to eat them in the presence of the Lord your God at the place the Lord your God will choose-you, your sons and daughters, your menservants and maidservants, and the Levites from your towns-and you are to rejoice before the Lord your God in everything you put your hand to. Be careful not to neglect the Levites as long as you live in your land.

Deuteronomy 14:22–29

Be sure to set aside a tenth of all that your fields produce each year. Eat the **tithe** of your grain, new wine and oil, and the firstborn of your flocks in the presence of the Lord your God at the place he will choose as a dwelling place for his Name, so that you may learn to revere the Lord your God always. But if that place is too distant and you have been blessed by the Lord your God and cannot carry your **tithe** (because the place where the Lord will choose to put his Name is so far away), then exchange your **tithe** for silver, and take the silver with you and go to the place the Lord your God will choose. Use the silver to buy whatever you like: cattle, sheep, wine or other fermented drink, or anything you wish. Then you and your household shall eat there in the presence of the Lord your God and rejoice. And do not neglect the Levites living in your towns, for they have no inheritance of their own.

At the end of every three years, bring all the **tithes** of that year's produce and store it in your towns, so that the Levites (who have no inheritance of their own) and the aliens, the fatherless and the widows who live in your towns may come and eat and be satisfied, and so that the Lord your God may bless you in all the work of your hands.

Deuteronomy 26:12–15

When you have finished setting aside a tenth of all your produce in the third year, the year of the **tithe**, you shall give it to the Levite, the alien, the fatherless and the widow, so that they may eat in your towns and be satisfied. Then say to the Lord your God: "I have removed from my house the sacred portion and have given it to the Levite, the alien, the fatherless and the widow, according to all you commanded. I have not turned aside from your commands nor have I forgotten any of them. I have not eaten any of the sacred portion while I was in mourning, nor have I removed any of it while I was unclean, nor have I offered any of it to the dead. I have obeyed the Lord my God; I have done everything you commanded me. Look down from heaven, your holy dwelling place, and bless your people Israel and the land you have given us as you promised on oath to our forefathers, a land flowing with milk and honey."

2 Chronicles 31:2–12

Hezekiah assigned the priests and Levites to divisions—each of them according to their duties as priests or Levites—to offer burnt offerings and fellowship offerings, to minister, to give thanks and to sing praises at the gates of the LORD's dwelling. The king contributed from his own possessions for the morning and evening burnt offerings and for the burnt offerings on the Sabbaths, New Moons and appointed feasts as written in the Law of the Lord. He ordered the people living in Jerusalem to give the portion due the priests and Levites so they could devote themselves to the Law of the Lord. As soon as the order went out, the Israelites generously gave the firstfruits of their grain, new wine, oil and honey and all that the fields produced. They brought a great amount, a **tithe** of everything. The men of Israel and Judah who lived in the towns of Judah also brought a **tithe** of their herds and flocks and a **tithe** of the holy things dedicated to the LORD their God, and they piled them in heaps. They began doing this in the third month and finished in the seventh month. When Hezekiah and his officials came and saw the heaps, they praised the Lord and blessed his people Israel.

Hezekiah asked the priests and Levites about the heaps; and Azariah the chief priest, from the family of Zadok, answered, "Since the people began to bring their contributions to the temple of the Lord, we have had enough to eat and plenty to spare, because the Lord has blessed his people, and this great amount is left over."

Hezekiah gave orders to prepare storerooms in the temple of the Lord, and this was done. Then they faithfully brought in the contributions, **tithes** and dedicated gifts. Conaniah, a Levite, was in charge of these things, and his brother Shimei was next in rank.

Nehemiah 10:37–39

Moreover, we will bring to the storerooms of the house of our God, to the priests, the first of our ground meal, of our grain offerings, of the fruit of all our trees and of our new wine and oil. And we will bring a **tithe** of our crops to the Levites, for it is the Levites who collect the **tithes** in all the towns where we work. A priest descended from Aaron is to accompany the Levites when they receive the **tithes,** and the Levites are to bring a tenth of the **tithes** up to the house of God, to the storerooms of the treasury. The people of Israel, including the Levites, are to bring their contributions of grain, new wine and oil to the storerooms where the articles for the sanctuary are kept and where the ministering priests, the gatekeepers and the singers stay.

"We will not neglect the house of our God."

Nehemiah 12:44

At that time men were appointed to be in charge of the storerooms for the contributions, firstfruits and **tithes**. From the fields around the towns they were to bring into the storerooms the portions required by the Law for the priests and Levites, for Judah was pleased with the ministering priests and Levites. (Neh. 12:44)

Nehemiah 13:4–5

Before this, Eliashib the priest had been put in charge of the storerooms of the house of our God. He was closely associated with Tobiah, and he provided him with a large room formerly used to store the grain offerings and incense and temple articles, and also the **tithes** of grain, new wine and oil prescribed for the Levites, singers and gatekeepers, as well as the contributions for the priests.

Nehemiah 13:10–12

I also learned that the portions assigned to the Levites had not been given to them, and that all the Levites and singers responsible for the service had gone back to their own fields. So I rebuked the officials and asked them, "Why is the house of God neglected?" Then I called them together and stationed them at their posts.

All Judah brought the **tithes** of grain, new wine and oil into the storerooms.

Amos 4:4–5

"Go to Bethel and sin; go to Gilgal and sin yet more. Bring your sacrifices every morning, your **tithes** every three years. Burn leavened bread as a thank offering and brag about your freewill offerings—boast about them, you Israelites, for this is what you love to do." declares the Sovereign Lord.

Malachi 3:8–11

"Will a man rob God? Yet you rob me.

"But you ask, 'How do we rob you?'

"In **tithes** and offerings. You are under a curse—the whole nation of you—because you are robbing me. Bring the whole **tithe** into the storehouse, that there may be food in my house. Test me in this," says the Lord Almighty, "and see if I will not throw open the floodgates of heaven and pour out so much blessing that you will not have room for it. I will prevent pests from devouring your crops, and the vines in your fields will not cast their fruit," says the Lord Almighty.

The word *tithe* appears fifteen times in the NIV Bible. The word *tithes* appears sixteen times. No other forms of the English word *tithe* appear. Although the word *tithe* does not appear in the New Testament, the word *tenth* does appear in passages understood to be concerning the tithe. All instances of the word *tenth* in the New Testament, as it applies to the tithe, will be covered in a later chapter (chapter 7, "Did Jesus Endorse the Tithe?").

2

What the Tithe Was

A tithe of everything from the land, whether grain from
the soil or fruit from the trees, belongs to the Lord.

—Leviticus 27:30

BEFORE WE EXPLORE what the tithe was, let's consider what
it is being taught today. First of all, the tithe is taught as
God's will for Christian giving. In modern-day American
mainstream Christianity, there are millions of little envelopes
that say Tithes and Offerings. So obviously, the tithe is not
some obscure doctrine of a particular denomination. The
tithe is something that many of us have grown up with as
part of the faith. The tithe is taught as 10 percent of your
monetary income. It is a common teaching that the first 10
percent of your income is supposed to be given away to your

local church. This first 10 percent pays the bills of running a church, generally. Offerings are different than tithes. An offering is a gift above and beyond the tithe. Offerings go to missions, special projects, holiday benevolence, etc. But it is generally discouraged that the tithe, that first 10 percent, goes anywhere but directly to the church. The tithe is taught as a matter of faith, discipline, and obedience. The tithe is taught as "putting God first" and is a demonstration of faithfulness in financial stewardship. Some go as far as to teach that even if money is tight and times are rough, you are still supposed to tithe in order to show God that you recognize Him as the source of your provision. Everyone who preaches the tithe has a slightly different view, but there are six widespread elements, or tenets, of the modern-day Christian tithe.

Six Tenets of Tithing

1. The tithe is different than offerings.
2. The tithe is money.
3. The tithe is a fixed 10 percent.
4. The tithe goes to your local church.
5. The tithe applies the same to everyone.
6. The tithe is still God's mandate for giving today.

Is the modern-day Christian practice of tithing consistent with what the tithe was to the Israelites as recorded in the Bible? *Absolutely not!* If you read the first chapter of this book, you probably read some things that surprised you. Let's examine how well these tenets of the modern-day tithe are in accordance with the original tithe(s) in Scripture.

The Tithe Is Different Than Offerings and the Tithe Is Money

The first two tenets are by far the easiest to deal with. Does the first tenet of tithing today match the biblical concept of the tithe? Yes, tithes and offerings are different. The Torah (the first five books of the Bible, also known as the "Law") is chock-full of the different kinds of offerings and detailed descriptions of them. So the contemporary practice matches the original practice in at least this regard. The second tenet of the modern-day tithe has no real basis in the letter of Scripture because the tithe was food, but I believe that it is true to the intent of Scripture. I believe the commandment to the Israelites was to share in what they produced with God. Only a few of us anymore produce food or livestock. Most of us produce money. And we share our money with God now instead of animals or grain. But of the six tenets, these are the only ones that are consistent with the biblical tithe in letter or intent.

The Tithe Is a Fixed 10 Percent

The third tenet of the modern-day tithe, and perhaps the most fundamental, does not match the original tithe as it is documented in the Bible or as practiced by the ancient

Israelites. The point in question is the percentage of an Israelite's annual income he was required to set aside in the form of a tithe. Naturally, the answer lies in the Bible. The Hebrew word *maser* is actually translated in English as both "tenth" and "tithe". Literally, a *maser* of anything meant a tenth of the total quantity. However, no matter how you interpret the Bible, the Israelites did not give away 10 percent of their annual incomes. In fact, what was actually practiced by the Jews, or at least espoused by the priesthood, was a system of three tithes. The first tithe, so-called the Lord's tithe or the Levites' tithe, was based on Leviticus 27:32 and Numbers 18:21–24. According to tradition, this is the tithe that went to the Levites every year because they had no means of making a living. The second tithe, or "festival tithe", was based on Deuteronomy 14:22–27. This tithe was for the purpose of funding the three sacred assemblies every year: Passover, the Feast of Tabernacles, and the Festival of Weeks. The third tithe, or the "poor's tithe", was based on Deuteronomy 14:28–29 and was meant to help the needy and the local Levite. The third tithe was only to be paid every three years. So under this system according to tradition, every Israelite was expected to set aside approximately[1] 23.3

1. These numbers represent a simplistic model of the Jewish cycle of years. For instance, this model neglects the Sabbath year, which was to have been observed every seven years. In theory, no tithes were supposed to be given or collected during this year. Factoring the Sabbath year into the model would lower the annual amount given away. But this is not the only complication in this cycle.

percent of his annual income in tithes. (The first two years he would pay 20 percent of his income in tithes, and the third year he would pay 30 percent. This averages to approximately 23.3 percent of his annual income.) An important quantity to consider (for the sake of the analysis further along in this book) is the amount that was expected to be given away in the three-tithe system. *In terms of the amount that was not kept for oneself, an Israelite was supposed pay roughly 13.3 percent of his income each year.*

While this system can be historically verified by numerous sources, I firmly believe that this was not God's intent. We see in the Gospels that there were two levels of Jewish "law". There was God's law as given in the Torah, and there was man's augmentation of it. The Pharisees not only followed God's law but also their own man-made extensions of the law. This can still be seen today in the laws of kosher food. The Bible says, "Do not cook a young goat in its mother's milk" (Exod. 23:19).

For some, this means one should not eat a cheeseburger. I am not claiming that "cheeseburger abstinence" is an invalid interpretation of the command in the Law, but I do wish

---

The year of Jubilee, an additional year of economic inactivity which was to have been observed every fifty years, would change these numbers yet again. For the sake of simplicity, limiting the discussion to only those years in which tithes were to be paid, the average annual amount set aside for tithes is around 23 percent according to the three-tithe interpretation of the Torah.

to point out that it is a notable extension of what is plainly written. Likewise, the religious leaders of Jewish antiquity took liberties in interpreting the passages on tithing. However, I do take issue with the traditional Jewish interpretation of the tithe, because I believe that those who expanded the tithe did so to their own profit.

It is important to reject the notion of an expanded three-tithe system for several reasons. For many pastors, this system forms the basis of the modern practice of tithing. In particular, there are people who, through the three-tithe interpretation, justify the idea that a flat 10 percent belongs to the church exclusively (tenets 3 and 4). However, I do not believe that the Bible supports this system. The reason to reject the three-tithe system, as I will demonstrate, is that it betrays God's original intent in prescribing the tithe to the Israelites. Modern Christianity has inherited and continued a practice that was first contaminated by the ancient Jewish priesthood. Once we understand God's original intent for the tithe, we can begin to think clearly about its place in the church today.

My first objection to the system of three tithes is based on the actual text of the Old Testament scriptures. Nowhere in the Bible does it say that there were supposed to be three tithes. This was an interpretation that was "read in" to the scriptures by the priests and rabbis of ancient Israel. To find this interpretation, one must look to extrabiblical Jewish writings to find evidence for a three-tithe system. To me, it's not that extrabiblical writings are to be dismissed outright.

Instead, the absence of an explicit reference within the Bible itself is peculiar given the nature of the Torah. In writings that are known for their exacting descriptions of rituals, practices, and physical objects, it seems odd that such a major feature of the system of required giving would be omitted.

It confounds me that the passage in Deuteronomy 14:22–29 would get broken up into two pieces representing two different tithes, when nothing in the text would suggest a distinction. When the word *tithe* is used in the sense of required giving, it is often preceded by the word *the*. This pronoun implies specificity. There is a big difference between *a* tithe and *the* tithe. The Bible does not refer to a "Levites'" tithe, or a "festival" tithe, or a "poor's" tithe. It was mankind who added the adjectives *Levites, festival*, and *poor's*. If the Old Testament translators have accurately conveyed the meaning of the text from Hebrew to English, "*the tithe*" means "*the only tithe*".

Consider Deuteronomy 26:12 (emphasis mine),

> When you have finished setting aside a tenth of all your produce *in the third year, the year of the tithe*, you shall give it to the Levite, the alien, the fatherless and the widow, so that they may eat in your towns and be satisfied.

What is meant by the phrase "the year of the tithe"? In the three-tithe system, this would refer to the third tithe, or the poor's tithe. However, I do not believe the third tithe is what was meant in Deuteronomy 26. I take this text at face value because this portion of Scripture was meant to be clear. Some portions of Scripture are intentionally mysterious (like the books of Daniel and Revelation). However, Deuteronomy is a book of instructions—and these were "revealed" in order to be followed.

> The secret things belong to the Lord our God, but the things revealed belong to us and to our children forever, that we may follow all the words of this law. (Deut. 29:29)

The Law was not written to confuse the Israelites. Interpreting the words in the Torah to create a three-tithe system is a clouding of a clear message.

Also consider Amos 4. As a background, throughout the book of Amos, God rebukes the Israelites for following the letter of the Law without pursuing the intent of the Law. The Israelites did many of the things they were commanded to do and yet continued in sin. The reference to the tithe in Amos is peripheral to its central message, but in it, we see God's intent for the tithe.

> "Go to Bethel and sin; go to Gilgal and sin yet more. Bring your sacrifices every morning, *your tithes every three years*. Burn leavened bread as a thank offering and brag about your freewill offerings—boast about them, you Israelites, for this is what you love

to do." declares the Sovereign Lord. (Amos 4:4–5; emphasis mine)

The prophet Amos quotes God as saying that He expected the tithes of Israel every three years. Moses didn't have to inform the people that they had to keep and eat the tithe in the other years. That was the easy part of tithing. The hard part was giving it away every three years, and this is what was stressed in these texts. It seems to me that the texts of the Old Testament, without the need for outside clues, are clear enough regarding the tithe being a single 10 percent being given away to the Levites every three years. However, there are more reasons than this to reject the notion of a three-tithe system.

My second objection to the system of three tithes is based on mathematics and the principle of fairness. The three-tithe system would have created a gross inequity of wealth among the Jews. In Numbers, appropriately, we find the distribution of the population among the tribes of Israel. The nonpriestly eleven tribes of Israel had the following populations of males twenty years or older at the time of the writing of the Torah according to Numbers 1.

Tribe	Population
Reuben	46,500
Simeon	59,300
Gad	45,650
Judah	74,600

Issachar	54,400
Zebulun	57,400
Joseph	72,700
Benjamin	35,400
Dan	62,700
Asher	41,500
Naphtali	53,400
Total	*603,550*

Unfortunately, the Bible does not list the number of Levite men twenty years and older; it only lists the total number of Levite males. There were twenty thousand total males according to Numbers 3. In America today, roughly 70 percent of the population is twenty or older. For the sake of the argument, let's be generous and say that 80 percent of the Levite males were twenty or older (this will minimize the estimate of the income of a Levite). That would give the Levites an analogous male population of 17,600.

Now let's consider the three-tithe system where the first tithe goes to the Levites every year. Let's assume that the average Israelite makes $50,000 a year and gives his first tithe, or $5,000, to the Levites (putting everything in modern comparison). This would mean that Israel as a whole would contribute just over $3 billion in tithes to the Levites. If the Levites shared in this revenue equally, that would mean that each Levite would have "as his inheritance" over $170,000 a year. (Remember, this number is a conservative estimate.) Each and every Levite would possess *over three times the wealth* of the Israelites he was called to "serve" under the three-tithe system. And on top of the first tithe, a portion of the third tithe also went to the local Levites (Deut. 14:29). Does this distribution seem like something God would have intended?

Let us forget any notion of a tithe for a second and consider what percentage would have been a fair amount for the Levites to receive. Let us also dust off our thinking caps and do a little story problem.

Story problem: What percentage of an Israelite's income should be taxed in order for a Levite to collect the same amount as the non-Levites?

Answer: $(17,600 \div 603,550) \times 100\% = 2.916\%$

This amount was easy to derive: it is simply the ratio of the population of the Levite tribe to the population of the other eleven tribes combined. At a rate of 2.916 percent collected from the rest of Israel, each Levite would collect $50,000 a year—the same as his brothers from the other tribes. Keep in mind that the Levites had to tithe on their income as well. The 10 percent that the Levites gave was strictly to be set aside for the Lord. Now if this tithe was the same as the tithe for the rest of Israel, the Levites would be required to give it every three years. In this system, the tithe would be enough to pay the Levites an equal share *and* give some away to the poor.

Consider what happened to the remainder of the 10 percent that the other eleven tribes paid every three years. If 3.333 percent was due to be paid in tithes on average and only

2.916 percent went to the Levites, how much would be left over for the widows and orphans? Actually, if you do the math (assuming an adult male population of six hundred thousand and an average income of $50,000), over $125 million a year would be made available to help out the neediest people. In a nation with an approximate total population of 1.6 million people (about the size of New Mexico), this seems like a lot of money made available strictly for state-sponsored aid. This figure is not counting any charity that might be given voluntarily on top of what was given in the tithe.

So what makes a whole lot more sense mathematically from a sense of fairness is what is plainly written in the Bible. There was one tithe that was to be used for different purposes. Every three years, it was to have been given away, establishing a society in which each tribe, including the Levites, got a fair share of the wealth. There was even enough left over for a significant amount to be given to the poor. Consequently, not only was this system fair, it was sufficient for charity as well. (Fairness and charity are very important themes in the book and will be addressed in detail later on.)

The conclusion I draw from all of this is that no matter how you interpret the Bible (i.e., a one-tithe system or a three-tithe system), the biblical tithe does *not* match what is preached today. I believe the Bible plainly teaches that the Levites shared in a tenth of the national income, so to speak, every three years. I believe I can safely say that this interpretation would have given rise to a system that was "just about right" for the nation of Israel. As you can probably imagine, the three-tithe system would have put a huge strain on Israel to line the purses of the Levites. But whether you believe that the Israelites *gave away* 3 or 13 percent of their annual incomes, there is no way that the modern practice is compatible with the biblical practice. The amount being taught today—a fixed 10 percent all the time—is artificial.

The Tithe Goes to Your Local Church

The next tenet of the modern-day tithe is that it belongs to your local church. Obviously, the beneficiaries of this money would be pastors and the physical structure often called the "church".

Concerning the modern-day Christian place of worship, there are many congregations who use the tithe as a building fund". You may be thinking that this is somehow similar to the way the ancient Jews used the tithe. You may be thinking that the three-tithe system (and this overkill of wealth) was necessary in order to maintain the buildings of the ancient Jewish faith—an analogue to the modern-day "building fund". There are two things which go against this thinking. One, the Bible does not say that the tithe was for the purpose of constructing or maintaining buildings. Two, this is not a practice which the Bible indicates that the Jews participated in. The major religious buildings of the Jewish faith, the Tabernacle and the Temple, were a result of one-time giving of the nation of Israel. In the case of the Tabernacle, it was strictly voluntary (Exod. 35, 36). In the case of the Temple, the effort to build it was mandated by Solomon (1 Kings 5). In both cases, though, the Jewish holy structures were built entirely using the resources available at the time of building. They were *not* built with the tithes. The purpose of the tithe as it pertains to the Temple, as you will recall from chapter 1, was storing food in it for the priests (2 Chron. 31, Neh. 12, Mal. 3). The Temple was *stocked* with the tithe (because the tithe was, by definition, food); it was not *built* with the tithe. Therefore, let us dismiss the notion that the tithe needed to be large in order to support building programs.

Concerning those in local ministry today, there are many churches which use the tithe to pay their pastors. The rationale for this is probably that today's pastors and the Levites of ancient Israel have many similarities. Both groups of people live in such a way that they do not participate in the national workforce; instead, they live a life of spiritual service to the people. It might be said that the modern pastor has "no inheritance of his own" just like the Levites. Hopefully, no pastor enters the field to make money. Rather, being a pastor is a noble profession which requires a calling from God and demands great responsibility. Pastors are called to visit hospitals, give eulogies, officiate wedding ceremonies, dedicate babies, and so on. They are God's representatives on earth, filling the role, practically speaking, in the new covenant that the Levites had in the old covenant. As such, they *deserve* the financial support of the people they serve. *But does God intend for their financial support to come from a modern-day "Christian" tithe?*

Again, nowhere in Scripture does it say that the Christian pastor is due the Levitical tithe. If you are still unconvinced that God's intent was a single tithe, and if you believe that the first of three tithes goes to your local church, then the percentages of the modern-day tithe and the Levites' tithe agree. They are both 10 percent. But what about the other tithes? If the first tithe is morally binding on the Christian, then so are the second and third tithes (if you believe that the Bible established a three-tithe system). But I, personally, have never heard any pastor say that not only are you to give 10 percent to your local church, you are to set aside 10 percent for yourself and another 3 percent (on average) for other charitable giving. This would be consistent with the three-tithe interpretation. On the other hand, if you agree with the idea that God's intent was a single tithe, then who receives the tithe is as important as the percentage associated with the tithe. Regardless of interpretation—whether one tithe or three tithes—I've never heard it taught that anything but the whole tithe belongs to the church. This is completely unbiblical. There were clearly three beneficiaries of the tithe in Scripture: the Levites, the poor, and *yourself*! The first time I read Deuteronomy 14, I was astounded. No one had ever taught me that I could (or should) spend the tithe on myself. I couldn't believe the words in front of me, *"Eat the tithe..."*

(Deut. 14:23; emphasis mine). Eat the tithe? I had always been taught that if you didn't give the tithe away, you were "robbing God". This is because all I had ever been taught about the tithe was a man-made invention in terms of who it rightfully belongs to. So we see that the modern teaching that the whole tithe belongs to the church is also a departure from God's original command.

The issue of how to support your local pastor is very important, and much of the latter half of this book is dedicated to addressing this issue. Let me state again that it is not the intent of this book to draw funds away from the local church and local pastors. But we as Christians need not go to the Old Testament as the basis for supporting Christian ministry. In fact, we should not go to the Old Testament to establish a Christian system of giving. There is a wealth of instruction in the New Testament on this matter that I will present later in the book.

The Tithe Applies the Same to Everyone

Another tenet of the modern-day tithe is that everyone must pay it, regardless of circumstance. The tithe applies universally to the rich and the poor, the employed and the unemployed, the clergy and the layman. I've heard it said that if you are down on your luck, you have an even greater cause to pay the tithe than usual. "You want God's blessing, don't you?" "You want God to open the storehouses of heaven in your life, don't you?" "If God can't trust you with a little, how can he trust you with a lot?" "Tithing will demonstrate to God that even in the worst of times, you acknowledge Him as the source of your provision and not any man or some earthly job." I've heard enough of this nonsense from actual preachers to make me sick to my stomach. Even the big, bad US government isn't this harsh. There is a level of relative poverty in which a person is not required to pay anything in the form of taxes. I believe God had something similar in mind when he wrote the Old Testament. He expressly told the Levites that they had to tithe on the tithes they received, but this commandment is absent from the other people who received the tithes: the poor, the fatherless, and the widows. If someone was poor enough to receive a portion of the tithe in ancient Israel, I think we can assume that it was okay for that person to keep all of it. Likewise, someone on welfare today shouldn't be expected to give a tenth of their income to the local church. I'm sure not all pastors who preach the tithe preach this aspect of it, but I have heard many who claim that the tithe is a tenth for everyone—and it belongs to God.

The Tithe Is Still God's Mandate for Giving Today

The idea that the tithe is still morally binding on Christians is the final tenet of the modern-day tithe. So far, I believe I have demonstrated that what is being taught and preached today as the tithe is different in many ways than what was prescribed in the Bible for the nation of Israel. The modern-day tithe is a contrivance, an artificial construct of Old Testament ideas in terms of the percentage that is given away, the people to whom it is given, and the people to whom it applies. In other words, the idea that Christians (as opposed to Israelites) must pay a fixed 10 percent (as opposed to 3 or 13 percent) to their local church (as opposed to the Levites) is an idea that is absent from Scripture. This is what I mean by "contrivance". Modern teachers have made up this idea, borrowing elements—a little here, a little there—from Scripture without being true or faithful to God's original intent for the tithe. You can see that the modern tithe is *similar* to the original biblical tithe, but these two systems of giving are clearly *not* the same.

So one might ask the question, "If the modern Christian tithe is so obviously inconsistent with the tithe of the Bible, is the tithe still God's mandate for giving today? And if so, what is the basis for it?" The next few chapters address these questions. Pastors and teachers have created clever, subtle, deceptive, and beguiling arguments to get Christians to believe that they must pay the biblical tithe. This is perhaps a little harsh, and to be fair, many of these pastors and teachers have themselves been deceived and are acting in good faith. However, I believe the criticism of modern pastors is deserved, because there is no excuse for a Christian leader to be ignorant of what is plainly written in Scripture, especially if he presumes to know enough to promote a practice (like tithing) using the Bible to justify it.

Therefore, in the following chapters, I tackle the arguments in favor of tithing head-on, using the same authority (the Bible) that these tithe preachers use to establish and justify a Christian tithe. You will see why terms like *clever* and *deceptive* fit the arguments put forward by tithe preachers as you understand what the Bible says on these topics. The purpose of the rest of this book is to annihilate the notion that the tithe is still morally binding on Christians. Indeed, the thesis of this work is that we, as Christians, are free to give in a manner which pleases the Spirit, not in a manner conforming to the written code of the Old Testament, and certainly not in a manner devised by man as some kind of hybrid of Old and New Testaments. As Jesus said, you cannot put new wine into old wineskins, and it will become clear throughout this book that God desires us to give in a new way, not in the way of the tithe.

Interlude 1

a time to tear down…

—Ecclesiastes 3:3

I assume you have read the passages in chapter 1 and you have thought through the arguments in chapter 2. With Scripture so obviously describing a different practice than what is preached today, how do preachers bridge the gap? How do you get from point A (the biblical tithe) to point B (the modern Christian tithe)? The next five chapters deal with common arguments in favor of a modern Christian tithe. Usually, preachers do not base the commandment to tithe on the justification "because I said so." Instead, modern pastors try to teach that tithing is not *their* own idea but that tithing is *God's* idea! These preachers use the Bible to convince their listeners that tithing is what God wants. Necessarily, we will be digging deep into the Bible to see if the arguments in favor of tithing pass the test of truth.

The following six arguments, in some form or another, seem to be the most pervasive arguments people use seriously to justify tithing. You will find these arguments listed at the beginning of the next five chapters. (Chapter 7 addresses two of the arguments.) For effect, I have set the text of these arguments in a different font (American Typewriter).

Argument 1: Tithing is binding on Christians because it is part of the Law that Christians still must follow.

Argument 2: Tithing is binding on Christians because of the precedent established by our spiritual forefather Abraham.

Argument 3: Abraham instituted the practice of tithing before the Law was established. Therefore, when the Law was canceled, it did not include the precedent or the practice of Abraham's tithe.

Argument 4: If you don't tithe, you are robbing God.

Argument 5: Jesus himself endorsed the tithe, and because it was a commandment of Christ, if for no other reason, Christians must tithe.

Argument 6: Jesus, as our High Priest, is due the tithe that has always been paid to God's priests. When the Law was changed from the old covenant law to the new covenant law, it meant that tithes are now due to Christ.

3

The Law

Now that faith has come, we are no longer
under the supervision of the Law.

—Galatians 3:25

He forgave us all our sins, having canceled
the written code, with its regulations, that
was against us and that stood opposed to us;
he took it away, nailing it to the cross.

—Colossians 2:14

For sin shall not be your master, because
you are not under law but under grace.

—Romans 6:14

Argument 1: Tithing is binding on Christians because it is part of the Law that Christians still must follow.

A very important aspect of any Christian doctrine is the relationship between the old and new covenants. The place in the Bible where the tithe is defined and instructions given for its observance is in the Old Testament. So the modern preacher in order to teach the tithe must connect the commandments of the old covenant to practices of the new covenant. Specifically, the tithe was included as part of the Mosaic law. So one might ask, "What is the relevance of the Mosaic law to the modern Christian?" One popular idea is that all commandments written in the Law are still binding for Christians unless specifically dismissed in the New Testament. Since tithing is not dismissed in the New Testament, those who believe this would say that it is still binding on Christians.

The truth (as testified by Scripture) is that the Mosaic law is completely nonbinding on Christians. You may never have been told that, but it's true. The Law *in its entirety was abolished* by Jesus Christ at Calvary. The evidence that Jesus abolished the Law is quite remarkable.

Consider the following three passages.

> Do not think that I have come to abolish the Law or the Prophets; I have not come to abolish them but to fulfill them. I tell you the truth, until heaven and

earth disappear, not the smallest letter, not the least
stroke of a pen, will by any means disappear from the
Law *until everything is accomplished*. (Matt. 5:17–18;
emphasis mine)

When he had received the drink, Jesus said, "*It is
finished.*" With that, he bowed his head and gave up
his spirit. (John 19:30; emphasis mine)

For he himself is our peace, who has made the
two one and has destroyed the barrier, the dividing
wall of hostility, by *abolishing in his flesh* the law with
its commandments and regulations. (Eph. 2:14–15;
emphasis mine)

Casually reading these passages may lead one to conclude
that the Bible contradicts itself. Jesus said he would not
abolish the Law in Matthew 5; Paul said he did abolish the
Law in Ephesians 2.

The connection between Matthew 5 and Ephesians 2
is what Jesus said on the cross as quoted in John. It is the
only Gospel that records Jesus saying, "It is finished." In the
English translation, it appears that Jesus is saying something
specific in "until everything is accomplished" and something
generic in "it is finished." But the opposite is true if we look
at the Greek words used for "accomplished" and finished".

The Greek word which was translated as "accomplished",
ginomai "γινομαι", was a common word and was most often
translated as a form of the English verb *to be*—was, is, be,

been, were, are, etc. It was also frequently translated as forms of the verb *to happen*. So Matthew 5:18 might have been translated as,

> I tell you the truth, until heaven and earth disappear, not the smallest letter, not the least stroke of a pen, will by any means disappear from the Law until everything *has happened*. (Matt. 5:18 [NIV modified]; change added in text)

The reason Jesus used such a generic word in his conditional "until" statement is because he was already speaking in the context of fulfillment of the Law. Other translations shed light on the original Greek to support this idea.

> Truly I tell you: so long as heaven and earth endure, not a letter, not a dot, will disappear from the Law until all that must happen has happened. (Matt. 5:18, REB)

> Amen, I say to you, until heaven and earth pass away, not the smallest letter or the smallest part of a letter, will pass from the Law until all things have taken place. (Matt. 5:18, NAB)

> In truth I tell you, till heaven and earth disappear, not one dot, not one stroke, is to disappear from the Law until its purpose is achieved. (Matt. 5:18, NJB)

So I believe Jesus was not saying that the Law would never be abolished; instead, he was saying that something must first happen with regard to fulfillment before the Law could be abolished. I believe Jesus revealed what must take place as he was dying (John 19:30). The NIV quotes Jesus as saying, "It is finished," but other translations quote him as saying, "It is accomplished," or "It is fulfilled."

The Greek word used in John 19:30 for "finished", *teleo* "τελεω", is actually a form of a word that found its way into the English language. The English word *teleology* has to do with studying phenomena, especially in nature, according to their purpose. *Teleological* is synonymous with *purposeful*. In the NIV, *teleo* is also translated as "fulfilled" and "accomplished." Unfortunately, when Jesus said, "It is finished," he did not say what "it" was. *Something* was finished, *teleo*, in the sense that it had served its purpose.

Paul clues us in to what "it" was. "It" was everything that needed to happen in order to abolish the Law. In Ephesians, we know that Jesus abolished the Law "in his flesh." As we all know from Communion, the significance of Jesus's flesh, or body, is that it was broken for us. This is a nice way to say that he was crucified. So Paul was saying that Jesus's death by crucifixion is what abolished the Law.

This truth came to humanity through a progressive revelation. First, Jesus said that the Law would be in effect until *something* happened. Then, as he was dying, he said that *something* was finished. Finally, Paul reveals that *the thing* that was finished was *the same thing* that had to happen in order to abolish the Law.

The application of this truth to the tithe is evident. I assert that because the tithe was part of the Law, it was abolished, and therefore, it is not binding on the Christian. However, there are some who disagree with me. They point out that circumcision, the Sabbath, animal sacrifice, kosher foods, ceremonial cleansing, and more have been specifically addressed and dismissed in the New Testament. Their idea is that the Old Testament is still the authoritative command from God and binding moral code unless otherwise noted in the New Testament. I am going to call this view the "Remnant Doctrine." I will call the adherents to this notion "Remnantists", because they believe there remains (thus the word *remnant*) a part of the Law which still applies to Christians. These Remnantists point out that lying, stealing, coveting, adultery, and cursing are all still sins. I once heard from a Remnantist, "Surely you don't think the Ten Commandments have been canceled, do you?" or something to that effect. They claim that nothing about Jesus's death changed these precepts. Their position is that because the New Testament writers did in fact make specific mention of the abolition of certain commands, this means the Law in general is still binding. They insist that specific commands would not need to be singled out for cancellation if the whole written code had indeed been canceled. With regards to the tithe, it was never explicitly canceled. In fact, in one of the few places the tithe is mentioned in the New Testament, Jesus himself validated the tithe (which is an argument we address in a later chapter). Therefore, based on the Remnant Doctrine, the tithe is still in effect.

I believe very strongly that the notion that there exists a remnant of the Law that is still binding (for Christians) is heresy and should be utterly rejected. If we follow the kind of reasoning employed by the Remnantists to its natural conclusion, then there has to be a list. Someone must have compiled "**The List**".

There was a lot written in the Old Testament. And most Christians are not Jews. We Gentiles have little knowledge of (primarily because we have had little training in) what was written for the Jews to observe. We see Orthodox Jews that have curly locks of hair coming from their temples. "Do not cut the hair on the sides of your head or clip the edges off your beard" (Lev. 19:27).

Was this nullified? Surely, with all of the hundreds of commandments stated in the Old Testament, there must be a list of which ones are in effect and which ones are not. Otherwise, how are we to know what is required of us? What if I have been sinning my whole life because I wear clothing made of blended fabrics? "Do not wear clothing woven of two kinds of material" (Lev. 19:19).

Which column in the List does this command go under, "binding" or "canceled"? *Search the Scriptures. See how many laws you violate!*

If these Remnantists are correct, then their idea has serious consequences for Christian doctrine and practice. It is easy for them to apply the Remnant Doctrine to one observance, but what they are saying applies to everything in the Law. Claiming that the tithe still binds because it was never canceled seems plausible. However, the effects of the Remnant Doctrine are far-reaching because the idea pertains to all of the Mosaic law.

Now the question is, "Is the Remnant Doctrine true?" Let us suppose that the Remnantists are correct. If they are, the New Testament is not enough to live by. In their scheme, the believer has the burden of figuring out what in the Old Testament is still mandated and what is not. If this is truly the case, then we must treat the Bible in the same way that lawyers and legislators treat civil law. We must extract the commandments in both Testaments, line them up against each other, and make a determination of the status of each command. Imagine going through that labor for the entire Old Testament! My point is that no one (at least that I am aware of) has bothered to complete that task. The status of the tithe is an easy chore to tackle because it is one command. But if these proponents of the tithe are correct, it is important to do this for all commands. If they would bother to do this, I think they would find out a couple of things. One, there is a lot more that still binds than they think. Two, their own lives would be in violation of many commandments that were never expressly dismissed in the New Testament.

The more important fact of the matter is that the Law cannot be broken into pieces and reassembled to form a new moral code. The Law exists in unity. It stands as a whole, and it falls as a whole. This idea of a partially binding moral code is nonsense. *There is no remnant.* God intended for the Law to be practiced in its entirety without exception. God spelled out blessings for obeying the Law and curses for breaking the Law. This was the covenant, or agreement, between God and the Israelites.

The Old Testament says,

> Cursed is the man who does not uphold the words of this law by carrying them out. (Deut. 27:26)

> If you fully obey the Lord your God and carefully follow *all* his commands I give you today, the Lord your God will set you high above all the nations of earth. (Deut. 28:1–2; emphasis added)

> However, if you do not obey the Lord your God and do not carefully obey *all* his commands

and decrees I am giving you today, all these curses will come upon you and overtake you. (Deut. 28:15; emphasis added)

The secret things belong to the Lord our God, but the things revealed belong to us and to our children forever, that we may follow *all* the words of this law. (Deut. 29:29; emphasis added)

And the New Testament says,

For whoever keeps the whole Law and yet stumbles at just one point is guilty of breaking all of it. (James 2:10)

Circumcision has value if you observe the Law, but if you break the Law, you have become as though you had not been circumcised. (Rom. 2:25)

All who rely on observing the Law are under a curse, for it is written: "Cursed is everyone who does not continue to do everything written in the Book of the Law." (Gal. 3:10; reference to Deut. 27:26)

Again I declare to every man who lets himself be circumcised that he is obligated to obey the whole Law. (Gal. 5:3)

Hopefully, you see that the Law really was (and still is) an all-or-nothing proposition. So even if we are talking about the time-honored Ten Commandments, they have been superseded by a new law. Not even the foundation of the Mosaic law, the most basic and fundamental part—the Ten Commandments, escapes being canceled by Christ's death. On the authority of the apostle Paul, we know,

> The commandments, "Do not commit adultery," "Do not murder," "Do not steal," "Do not covet," and whatever other commandment there may be, are summed up in this one rule: "Love your neighbor as yourself." Love does no harm to its neighbor. Therefore love is the fulfillment of the law. (Rom. 13:9–10)

Paul explicitly lists four of the Ten Commandments in Romans 13:9. He lumps these core commandments of the Jewish faith with "*whatever other commandment there may be.*" So it is not merely the opinion of the author that the entire Law has been canceled and replaced. I am not saying anything that Scripture does not also say explicitly. But how can this be? you might ask. I can well imagine a reader thinking that I am proposing some new idea or concept in violation of traditional Christian teaching. But this isn't the case. Read Galatians and Hebrews again carefully. This is a fundamental truth of the New Testament stated over and over again. Therefore, none of us has to worry about which parts of the Old Testament are binding on believers in Christ.

Like Jews, Christians shouldn't lie, steal, covet, swear, etc. Please understand my point in saying the Mosaic law has been canceled. It doesn't mean "anything goes". The creed of Satanism is, "Do what thou wilt." This is *not* what I am espousing. I'm saying that Christians avoid stealing not because there is an explicit law against it; instead, Christians don't steal because it would violate the universal law of love. How many laws would it take to make sure every bad behavior was prohibited? Count how many commandments there are in the Old Testament. You should find 613 of them! I remind my Christian audience that Jesus gave us one Law (*love*—an imperative verb) in two parts—(1) love God and (2) love humanity (Matt. 22:36–40). This is what Paul in Romans 13:9 was simply reiterating. This is a pretty easy list to remember. If only the List was so easy to obey!

In conclusion, I hope I have made it clear that the Mosaic law, in its entirety, is no longer in effect for the blood-bought, born-again, Spirit-filled believer. Because the tithe was a commandment in the Law, the cancellation of the Law is strong evidence against a modern-day tithe. But *even if* Christians are supposed to tithe, it means there must be some other reason than "the tithe is part of the Law that wasn't canceled." Hopefully, now you are equipped to see through this baseless argument in favor of tithing.

4

Abraham, Melchizedek, and Jesus

Then Abram gave him a tenth of everything.

—Genesis 14:20

You are a priest forever, in the order of Melchizedek.

—Psalm 110:2, Hebrews 7:17

If you belong to Christ, you are Abraham's
seed, and heirs according to the promise.

—Galatians 3:29

Argument 2: Tithing is binding on Christians
because of the precedent established by
our spiritual forefather Abraham.

Many advocates of tithing use Abraham as the reason why Christians should tithe. According to these advocates, Abraham is important for both *what* he did and *when* he did it. This chapter addresses the *what*, and the next chapter addresses the *when* as it pertains to the precedent set by Abraham.

I once sat in the presence of a preacher who made this argument: "Abraham tithed to Melchizedek. We are the seed of Abraham. Jesus is the priest in the order of Melchizedek. Therefore, we must tithe to Jesus."

Another rendering of this argument is that Abraham established a precedent that we, his spiritual offspring, are required to keep. Following this line of reasoning, that precedent was the practice of the tithe, which we maintain by giving 10 percent of our income to the local church. In similar manner as chapter 2, let us examine Scripture to see if what Abraham did was in any way congruous with what is being taught today as the tithe.

Before we study Abraham's actions, with whom most everyone is familiar, I will give a little background on Melchizedek, who is not so well-known. Melchizedek is mentioned in only three places in the Bible: Genesis 14, Psalm 110, and Hebrews 6 and 7. (I strongly encourage the reader to become acquainted again with these passages before continuing in this chapter.) In fact, most of what we know about Melchizedek comes from the author of Hebrews (whom I believe and assume to be Paul).

Paul writes the following concerning Melchizedek:

> This Melchizedek was king of Salem and priest of God Most High. He met Abraham after the defeat of the kings and blessed him, and Abraham gave him a tenth of everything. First, his name means "king of righteousness"; then also, "king of Salem" means "king of peace". Without father or mother, without genealogy, without beginning of days or end of life, like the Son of God he remains a priest forever.
>
> Just think how great he was: Even the patriarch Abraham gave him a tenth of the plunder! Now the Law requires the descendents of Levi who become priests to collect a tenth from the people—that is, their brothers—even though their brothers are descended from Abraham. This man, however, did not trace his descent from Levi, yet he collected a tenth from Abraham and blessed him who had the promises. And without a doubt, the lesser person is blessed by the greater. In the one case, the tenth is collected by men who die; but in the other case by him who is declared to be living. One might even say that Levi, who collects the tenth, paid the tenth through Abraham, because when Melchizedek met Abraham, Levi was still in the body of his ancestor. (Heb. 7:1–10)

This passage can be very confusing. It is as if Paul is saying that there is another Christ out there that we were not aware of. The description of Melchizedek in Hebrews 7:3 and 7:8 seems to indicate that he is a god. In fact, there are cults that worship Melchizedek based on these words. However, there is an alternative interpretation of Hebrews 7:3 and 7:8 that is more compatible with the rest of Scripture.

It is the consensus of Christian biblical scholars that, in writing to the Hebrews, the author was employing a literary device known to the Hebrews. It is known as the "argument from silence", and it is based on the notion that if something is not recorded in Scripture, then it never happened. Genesis, as you know, is a very detailed account of the descent of the Jews from the original Adam. There is an unbroken chain of human lineage from God's first man to the incarnation of Israel as a man (Jacob), a family (his twelve sons), and the nation that bears his name. Genesis comprises the "who's who" in the family tree of Israel. But there was one man, a very important man, who was not included in any genealogy in Genesis or anywhere else in the Bible. This man was the King of Salem (literally, "peace", and also Jerusalem), as well as the priest of the Most High God. This man was known as "Melchizedek", and in accordance with the principle of silence, he had no mother or father because they were not mentioned. He was never born and never died, because it was not mentioned. And his priesthood continues forever, because its cessation is not mentioned. In a modern essay, Paul would say that Melchizedek had no *recorded* genealogy, or mother or father. Paul would say that in a book of records,

Melchizedek was without *recorded* death or birth. In Genesis, Melchizedek appears on the scene abruptly, with zero background information, as the spiritual authority on the earth, even greater than Abraham. And he disappears from the narrative passages of the entire Old Testament afterward. He is only mentioned afterward in one phrase in Psalms in a prophecy concerning the Messiah.

What is very interesting about Melchizedek is that he was not a Jew. Again, according to the argument from silence, Melchizedek was not related to Abraham because Genesis does not mention it. Only those who descended from Jacob (Israel) and thus Abraham can be called Jews. So God's ordained priest during Abraham's lifetime might be considered a Gentile. Maybe more appropriately, the categories "Jew" and "Gentile" do not apply to Melchizedek because he predated Jacob. Either way, we see the parallel to the priesthood of Jesus. Jesus is the priest of all mankind, not just the Jews, just as Melchizedek was. This is in contrast to the priesthood of the Levites (in the order of Aaron) established later in history, which was a specific ministry of the Jews, by the Jews, and for the Jews exclusively. The Law made clear that one could only become a priest by birthright. But the priesthood of Jesus and Melchizedek was based on a divine appointment and their superior moral character. The book of Hebrews declares that Christians are not subordinate to the Levitical priesthood nor are we under the authority of the law on which the priesthood was based. Instead, the message in

Hebrews to Christians everywhere is that Jesus is a superior priest, like Melchizedek, of a new and better covenant. This new covenant is the *good news* humanity has been waiting for.

Now that we have a little background on Melchizedek and his significance to Christianity, we can put Abraham's actions in a more proper perspective. Let's read the account in Genesis concerning Abraham and Melchizedek.

> When Abram heard that his relative [Lot] had been taken captive, he called out the 318 trained men in his household and he went in pursuit as far as Dan. During the night Abram divided his men to attack them [Kedorlaomer, the king of Elam; Tidal, king of Goiim; Amraphel, king of Shinar; and Arioch, king of Ellasar—Gen. 14:9] and he routed them, pursuing them as far as Hobah, north of Damascus. He recovered all the goods and brought back his relative Lot and his possessions, together with the women and the other people.
>
> After Abram returned from defeating Kedorlaomer and the kings allied with him, the King of Sodom came out to meet him in the Valley of Shaveh (that is, the King's Valley).
>
> Then Melchizedek king of Salem brought out bread and wine. He was priest of God Most High, and he blessed Abram, saying, "Blessed be Abram by God Most High, Creator of heaven and earth. And blessed be God Most High, who delivered your enemies into your hand." Then Abram gave him a tenth of everything. (Gen. 14:14–20)

From this passage, it is easy to see why Paul wrote using the argument from silence. This is the only narrative passage concerning Melchizedek in the entire Bible, so there is obviously not a lot of information. The sum total of information we have on Melchizedek is contained in just three sentences! Notice that Abraham was not called "Abraham" yet in this passage. Perhaps Abram would not have become "Abraham" if Melchizedek had not blessed him.

Genesis 14 is the first time in the Bible that the Hebrew word *maser* is used. This account is significant to many because of the "principle of first mention". Many Bible scholars believe that there is special insight to be gained from a study of the first time a word or a concept is introduced in Scripture. This is why it is important to understand what happened between Abraham and Melchizedek no matter what your position on tithing is.

So let's now look a little closer at this word *maser* and the first time it is used in Scripture. There happens to be another word used in Hebrew scriptures, *siyriy*, which means "tenth" in a more generic mathematical sense. As far as I can tell in the research that I have been able to do (and I highly encourage the reader to check me on this), *maser* (usually translated as "tithe") carried additional significance that *siyriy* (usually translated as "tenth") did not. The word *maser* usually denoted a tribute—a payment of some kind in gratitude and in deference to a superior or respected entity (like a king or a priest). Apparently, payment of this special "tenth" to men of high esteem was a common practice in the ancient world. The point I want to make is that while *maser* literally means tenth, the emphasis of the word *maser* (versus *siyriy*) was its significance as a tribute. Now that we see the subtle shades of meaning for the word *maser* we can see how it fits both the account of Abraham in Genesis 14 as well as the passages which describe the tithe later in the Bible.

Interestingly, there are not many similarities between Abraham's tribute to Melchizedek and the modern-day tithe. Keep in mind that many pastors point to this original event as the precedent for the modern-day tithe. But what was the precedent? First of all, Abraham gave his tribute *voluntarily*. Obviously, there is not a lot to go on, but I think I'm being true to the text in Genesis to state that Abraham was not required to give anything to Melchizedek. It is implied that Abraham gave as a token of gratitude for the blessing Melchizedek pronounced over him. By contrast, the tithe is required to be given. Secondly, Abraham gave his tithe as a one-time occurrence. Again, with the information before us on this matter, we cannot conclude that Abraham gave regularly to Melchizedek. The Bible is silent except to say that the giving of the tenth happened *once*. On the other hand, the tithe is to be given regularly. Finally, Abraham did not even give away what was his to begin with. This is the biggest departure from the tithe. In Genesis, it is unclear just what Abraham had in his possession after defeating his enemies. Did he recover just that which belonged to Lot and the other captives? Or in routing the four kings, did Abraham take what belonged to his enemies as well? I believe Genesis itself implies that Abraham was carrying the spoils of war, but this is confirmed in the book of Hebrews, "Abraham gave him a tenth of the plunder!" (Heb. 7:4).

Abraham gave away wealth that did not belong to him. How does this in any way establish the precedent for the modern-day tithe? In the modern-day tithe, you give a tenth of your own wealth, certainly not the wealth of someone else. In my view, the precedent being set is that if a pastor blesses you and that week you win the lottery, then you should give a tenth of the winnings back to him. I surely do not see any pattern being set in terms of a Christian giving to Jesus by the account in Genesis.

In conclusion, it seems to me that exhorting people to tithe based on the deeds of Abraham is an odd way to approach Christian giving. There is an inconsistency between the example set by Abraham and the goal of the proponents of a modern-day tithe. The pastors in America do not want their sheep to be one-time givers. They do not want the flock to give away only that which is above and beyond their normal income. The proponents of a modern-day tithe want regular, faithful, and sacrificial givers. Abraham may have been all of the above, but this is *not* what happened between him and Melchizedek. If Christians represent Abraham and Jesus represents Melchizedek, and the model for Christian giving is Genesis 14, then what results is *anything but* what is taught as the tithe today.

5

Before the Law

Abraham, Tithing, and Circumcision

> The Law, introduced 430 years later, does not set aside
> the covenant previously established by God.
>
> —Galatians 3:17

Argument 3: Abraham instituted the practice of tithing before the Law was established. Therefore, when the Law was canceled, it did not include the precedent or the practice of Abraham's tithe.

While the previous chapter dealt with *what* Abraham did, this chapter will deal with *when* he did it. Some proponents of the tithe believe it is in effect today because it was instituted with Abraham, before the Mosaic law, and therefore was not abolished when the new covenant was established.

But first, for the sake of thoroughness, let's examine the only other time that a "tenth" is mentioned before the establishment of the Law as it pertains to giving. This incident involves Jacob, Abraham's grandson. During Jacob's flight from Esau, on his way to Laban, Jacob promised to remember God's provision and protection.

> Then Jacob made a vow, saying, "If God will be with me and will watch over me on this journey I am taking and will give me food to eat and clothes to wear so that I safely return to my father's house, then the Lord will be my God and this stone that I have set up as a pillar will be God's house, and of all that you give me I will give you a tenth." (Gen. 28:20–22)

This is, by far, a superior precedent than the one set by Abraham. First of all, it is a premeditated and direct promise to God, not an extemporaneous act toward a man. Secondly, the promise concerns "all" of Jacob's income, not just the load he was carrying. Thirdly, the promise concerns giving God back what He would provide, not the stolen belongings of a defeated enemy. Jacob's tenth sounds a lot more like the modern tithe than Abraham's tenth.

Mysteriously, Jacob's example is mentioned very rarely when it comes to tithing. If we follow the line of reasoning employed in the argument involving Abraham, then,

Jacob, or "Israel", tithed to God.
Christians are a part of "Israel" (Rom. 2, Rom. 11).
Therefore, Christians must tithe to God.

I have to admit that I have not heard anyone use this argument. It seems odd to me that while many use Abraham as a precedent for tithing, no one uses Jacob—except for one thing. Jacob, in his vow, puts a condition on God first, then on himself. This is the one glaring feature of Jacob's tenth that excludes it from being taken seriously, I suppose, as an example of tithing before the Law. The modern-day tithe is taught to be this: you give the first part of your income, and then God blesses you and the remaining 90 percent. Often, the words *tithe* and *first fruits* are used interchangeably by the proponents of a modern-day tithe. Jacob, it seemed, was going to give his "fruits" *after* God blessed him.

There is not much I can expound on concerning Jacob's tenth. It seems to be a nonissue for both sides of the tithing debate. I chose to include it for the sake of future reference and general instruction for the reader, but for the rest of this chapter, I will address the precedent set by Jacob's grandfather, Abraham, since that is the one referred to almost exclusively by preachers of the modern-day tithe.

Regardless of which patriarch is considered the originator of the Christian tithe, it is important that we confront the argument that the tithe is still in place because it was established before the giving of the Law.

There was another significant precedent set by Abraham long before the law of Moses was established: circumcision.

> Then God said to Abraham, "As for you, you must keep my covenant, you and your descendents after you for the generations to come. This is my covenant with you and your descendents after you, the covenant you are to keep: Every male among you shall be circumcised. You are to undergo circumcision, and it will be a sign of the covenant between me and you. For the generations to come every male among you who is eight days old must be circumcised, including those born in your household or bought with money from a foreigner—those who are not your offspring. Whether born in your household or bought with your money, they must be circumcised. *My covenant in your flesh is to be an everlasting covenant.* Any uncircumcised male, who has not been circumcised in the flesh, will be cut off from his people; he has broken my covenant. (Gen. 17:9–14; emphasis mine)

Here we see that God took the covenant of circumcision very seriously. The implied penalty for breaking this covenant is death. The relevant feature of this "everlasting covenant" is that it was explicitly established before the giving of the Law.

Those who say that the tithe was instituted before the giving of the Law point to this passage in Scripture. (I include it again because I want to highlight that this passage is qualitatively different than the passage relating to circumcision.)

> After Abram returned from defeating Kedorlaomer and the kings allied with him, the king of Sodom came out to meet him in the Valley of Shaveh (that is, the King's Valley). Then Melchizedek king of Salem brought out bread and wine. He was priest of the God Most High, and he blessed Abram, saying, "Blessed be Abram by God Most High, Creator of heaven and earth. And blessed be God Most High, who delivered your enemies into your hand."
>
> Then Abram gave him a tenth of everything. (Gen. 14:17–20)

In Genesis 17, circumcision was explicitly decreed by God. However, in Genesis 14, God is not reported to have participated directly in the exchange between Abram and Melchizedek. The part mentioning a "tenth" is an account of an act that occurred in history. There is nothing in this text to suggest that any practice was instituted. The passage concerning the tithe in Numbers is much more similar in character to the passage in Genesis concerning circumcision.

> "I give to the Levites all the tithes in Israel as their inheritance in return for the work they do while

serving in the Tent of Meeting. From now on the Israelites must not go near the Tent of Meeting, or they will bear the consequences of their sin and die. It is the Levites who are to do the work at the Tent of Meeting and bear the responsibility for offenses against it. *This is a lasting ordinance for the generations to come.* They will receive no inheritance among the Israelites. Instead, I give to the Levites as their inheritance the tithes that the Israelites present as an offering to the Lord. That is why I said concerning them: 'They will have no inheritance among the Israelites.'" (Num. 18:21–24; emphasis mine)

And now I would like to point out the similarities and differences between circumcision and tithing. They are similar in that the first mention of both practices is with Abraham in Genesis. The practices are similar in that they are both described as *olam*. This word is translated as "everlasting" with respect to circumcision and as "lasting" in regard to tithing. The definite implication of the Hebrew term *olam* is permanence. They are slightly different in that circumcision was called a "covenant" and tithing was called an "ordinance". However, they were both very much commandments of God that were meant to be obeyed in Hebrew culture. The practices are again slightly different in terms of when they were officially established. Circumcision was officially established with Abraham (Gen. 17:13; the text I put in *italic*). Tithing was officially established with Moses (Num. 18:23; the text I put in *italic*). However, again both were still commandments of God that eventually got lumped together as integral parts of Hebrew culture and law. A more significant difference between the practices is the level of treatment they receive in the Law. Tithing is given extensive and explicit treatment in the Law (Lev. 27, Num. 18, Deut. 12, 14, 26). Circumcision is almost absent from the Law. It is only mentioned in two places. In Exodus 12, Moses commands that anyone who observes Passover be circumcised. In Leviticus 12, Moses restates that circumcision is to be performed on the eighth day after birth. Other than that, no other commandment is given in the Law concerning circumcision.

As you can see, tithing and circumcision are close cousins. They both originated with Abraham. They were both called *olam* by God. They were both instituted as essential practices in Jewish law and Hebrew culture. If, as according to some, the tithe was instituted before the giving of the Law and thus still in effect, shouldn't circumcision share the same status as the tithe—that is, still in effect?

Obviously, the debate over circumcision is a famous one and appears numerous times in the New Testament. In fact, the English word *circumcision* appears more often in the texts of the New Testament than the Old Testament!

From the beginning, some of the early Jewish Christians believed that circumcision was still binding on Gentile Christians.

Then some of the believers who belonged to the party of the Pharisees stood up and said, "The Gentiles must be circumcised and required to obey the Law of Moses." (Acts 15:5)

This idea was addressed by Peter and the rest of the council at Jerusalem in Acts 15:6–31. This passage is too lengthy to quote here, but I encourage you to read this passage and witness the reasoning the apostles employed to dispel the idea that Christians should be circumcised.

Of course, if anyone was opposed to the idea of Christian circumcision, it was Paul. He addressed the topic quite emphatically in his epistles.

Circumcision has value if you observe the Law, but if you break the Law, you have become as though you had not been circumcised. If those who are not circumcised keep the Law's requirements, will they not be regarded as though they were circumcised? The one who is not circumcised physically and yet obeys the Law will condemn you who, even though you have the written code and circumcision, are a lawbreaker. (Rom. 2:25–27)

Was a man uncircumcised when he was called? He should not be circumcised. Circumcision is nothing and uncircumcision is nothing. Keeping God's commands is what counts. (1 Cor. 7:18–19)

Mark my words! I, Paul, tell you that if you let yourselves be circumcised, Christ will be of no value to you at all. Again I declare to every man who lets himself be circumcised that he is obligated to obey the whole Law. You who are trying to be justified by law have been alienated from Christ; you have fallen away from grace. But by faith we eagerly await through the Spirit the righteousness for which we hope. For in Christ Jesus neither circumcision nor uncircumcision has any value. The only thing that counts is faith expressing itself through love. (Gal. 5:2–6)

Those who want to make a good impression outwardly are trying to compel you to be circumcised. The only reason they do this is to avoid being persecuted for the cross of Christ. Not even those who are circumcised obey the Law, yet they want you to be circumcised that they may boast about your flesh. May I never boast except in the cross of our Lord Jesus Christ, through which the world has been crucified to me, and I to the world. Neither circumcision nor uncircumcision means anything; what counts is a new creation. (Gal. 6:12–15)

Now if you are like me, some of what Paul says (at least on the surface) seems illogical. In one sentence, Paul states that "Keeping God's commands is what counts." I can imagine someone thinking, *Since **when** is circumcision not a command of God? It is an **everlasting** covenant!* But you've got to ask yourself, "God's commands *to whom*?" God never gave the command to Gentiles to be circumcised. If all of Scripture applies to everybody, Paul is stupid—or worse. But Paul was not stupid or wicked, and therefore, Paul's admonition to the Gentiles to keep God's commands was obviously in reference to something other than the Torah. Otherwise, "keeping God's commands" would mean observing the practice of circumcision. Let's think for a minute, then. If Paul wasn't talking about Old Testament law as "God's commands", what was he talking about? Let me just say that if you meditate on that question, you'll realize the truth about tithing and *much* more.

Reading Paul from the perspective that Old Testament commandments don't apply to Christians (as we know from chapter 3) sheds light on his reasoning processes. He's not being illogical at all. He simply understands the differences between the distinct covenants God made with man. He confronted Jewish Christians when they *illogically* tried to impose laws from the Jewish covenants that had no bearing on Gentile believers in Christ. Whether Paul is guilty of being illogical or not, he was unambiguously clear that circumcision is not binding on Christians. Notice that even though it was instituted *before* the Law, Paul includes it *with* the Law. Therefore, when the written code was canceled, this canceled circumcision as well.

So how can "Abraham's tithe" be any different than circumcision? If "Abraham's everlasting covenant" is canceled, how can the much weaker precedent of "Abraham's tithe" remain intact? It cannot, and we now see that the argument in favor of tithing based on the precedent of Abraham is hopelessly flawed. The problem is that the argument applies equally well to both circumcision and tithing. When we consider the spiritual principles Paul taught us concerning circumcision, we see that these same principles also nullify tithing. Hopefully, now you are equipped to handle any argument in favor of tithing based on the deeds of Abraham.

6

Malachi 3

Giving Under Compulsion

"Will a man rob God? Yet you rob me. But you ask,
'How do we rob you?' In tithes and offerings. You are
under a curse—the whole nation of you because you are
robbing me. Bring the whole tithe into the storehouse,
that there may be food in my house. Test me in this,"
says the Lord Almighty, "and see if I will not throw open
the floodgates of heaven and pour out so much blessing
that you will not have room enough for it. I will prevent
pests from devouring your crops, and the vines in your
fields will not cast their fruit," says the Lord Almighty.

—Malachi 3:8–11

Argument 4: If you don't tithe, you are robbing God.

This argument may be the simplest of all arguments in favor of tithing, but it is probably the most effective. However, as you will see, it is also probably the most transparently flawed argument in favor of tithing. You will also see that it is not the people who disregard the tithe who violate God's commands but it is the pastors who compel their flocks to tithe based on Malachi 3 who are sinning.

The third chapter of Malachi is the most recognized passage on tithing in the Bible. The passage is really quite extraordinary. God's rebuke of the Israelites is particularly clear and direct. It is the only place in the Bible where God condones that people actually test Him, and the promised blessings are almost unparalleled. These verses provide the most compelling material for preachers of the modern-day tithe. They say, on the authority of Scripture, that to withhold the tithe is stealing. No God-fearing person wants to be considered a thief, a spiritual criminal.

By now, hopefully at this point in the book, we can see the truth regarding this passage. There is absolutely no place for this passage in Christianity. First of all, the "tithe" Malachi spoke of is not the one being preached today. But more importantly, again, we come to the point where we, as Christians, must realize that we are not under the Law of the Old Testament. In light of this, we see that God simply was not talking to Christians in Malachi 3!

I learned this truth the hard way, and I think you'll be both entertained and edified by the following story of something which really happened in my life. I attended a church that issued a "Ninety-Day Tithe Challenge". They based this challenge on the promises of scripture from Malachi 3:10. We were supposed to tithe for ninety days and "test God" as Scripture says. At the end of ninety days, if we hadn't been blessed in miraculous ways, we could stop tithing. I decided to put God and His promises in Scripture to the test. I had been tithing sporadically, so I determined that I would (for ninety days) tithe my income exactly as the church told me to. My expectation (as influenced by my pastors) was that the 90 percent of my remaining income would go farther than if I had kept all 100 percent to myself. Being the math guy that I am, I knew that for 90 percent to go farther than 100 percent, something extraordinary must happen. Particularly, I was looking for great bargains on the things I normally spent money on. I was expecting (in faith!) that when I would go to the store for toothpaste (for example), I would find that the toothpaste I wanted was on sale.

As soon as I started taking this challenge, I seemed to possess an uncanny knack for *missing* these sales I was looking for. I remember missing an airline fare sale by a couple of days that amounted to a fairly significant sum of money—several hundred dollars, I think. The savings (that I missed) on the airline tickets would have more than covered the amount I had tithed for that paycheck. I became furious.

This is precisely the kind of thing "they" (my church, God, the Bible) promised me wouldn't happen. This, in my opinion, was a major counterexample to receiving "so much blessing that you will not have room enough for it."

This experience really affected me. I was mad at God. It made me seriously question the validity of Scripture. I went into the deal with the idea that my own disobedience had been holding me back from God's blessing. With sincerity of heart and with hope and faith, I sought to honor the Ninety-Day Tithe Challenge, but instead, I became completely disillusioned.

To make a long story short, I eventually realized that the Holy Spirit conspired against me and the Ninety-Day Tithe Challenge in order to show me even greater truths about giving. As a result of this experience, I realized the central thesis of this book: we are free to give in the way of the Spirit, not in a manner conforming to the written code of the Old Testament. But even more importantly, I learned something about God. He really does care about our relationship with Him. And He will frustrate your attempts to serve Him if your service is not based in truth. God was more concerned that I knew His true character than He was with fulfilling what I thought (erroneously) were His promises to me. The experience was damaging for a season, but it deepened my relationship with God in the long run.

As for the blessings and curses of Malachi 3 (the basis of the Ninety-Day Tithe Challenge), I was shown that the

Christian has no concern. To us, the Law is dead. We live by the Spirit, not the Law. Malachi 3 is nailed to the cross with the rest of the old code. Even so, Christian pastors still compel their flocks to give the tithe using Malachi 3:8–11. And I firmly believe that those pastors, preachers, and teachers who compel their audiences to tithe based on Malachi 3 are acting in violation of the will of God.

But is it really *compulsion* to tell someone to tithe based on Malachi 3? Admittedly, *compulsion* is a strong word. But, in my opinion, it is a word that aptly fits what pastors are doing by telling their flocks they are "robbing God". I call this tactic, this guilt trip, by a trusted person in authority *compulsion*. The English words *compel*, *compulsory*, and *compulsion* are all related. In both the *Webster*'s and *Random House* dictionaries of the English language, these words have to do with the applying of force to accomplish something. When these words are used in the Greek in the New Testament, they are also related. The words *ananké* "αναγκη" and *anankazó* "αναγκαζω" are translated "need", "necessary", "compel", "compelled", "compulsion", "force", "forced", "crisis", "drove to it", "must", "make", "made", etc. The Greek word *anankazo* appears twice in Galatians where Paul writes on the topic of non-Jewish Christians being taught that they must undergo circumcision.

> Yet not even Titus, who was with me, was *compelled* [anankazo] to be circumcised, even though he was a Greek. This matter arose because some false brothers

had infiltrated our ranks to spy on the freedom we have in Christ Jesus and to make us slaves. We did not give in for a moment, so that the truth of the gospel might remain with you. (Gal. 2:3–5)

Those who want to make a good impression outwardly are trying to *compel* [anankazo] you to be circumcised. The only reason they do this is to avoid being persecuted for the cross of Christ. (Gal. 6:12)

In the previous chapter, we saw that Paul nullifies circumcision as a practice in Romans and 1 Corinthians. Here in Galatians, he condemns those who preach circumcision as being compulsory (*anankazo*) or required. So, according to Paul, it is wrong to compel someone to engage in a practice which is not spiritually binding on that person. Specifically, he singled out circumcision in several places. But doesn't the principle here apply more broadly than just circumcision?

In the last chapter, I pointed out some similarities between the practices of tithing and circumcision. The analogy becomes more complete when we look at Paul's teaching on giving under compulsion. With regard to giving, he says,

Each man should give what he has decided in his heart to give, not reluctantly or under *compulsion* [ananke], for God loves a cheerful giver. (2 Cor. 9:7)

Given what we know about the relationship between the tithe, the Law, and circumcision, this is the only conclusion which is consistent with the rest of Paul's teachings. Paul uses variants of the same root word, *anankazo* and *ananke*, when dismissing mandatory circumcision as well as mandatory giving. Therefore, closer inspection of the text itself in 2 Corinthians 9 shows that it cannot be reconciled with Malachi 3.

So how do modern-day tithe preachers resolve the conflict between Malachi 3 and 2 Corinthians 9? I have actually posed this question to preachers. The response: "Pay the tithe cheerfully!" But to say this is to ignore Paul. There is no reconciliation between giving what you have *decided in your heart* and giving what is *required by the law.* I tell you that anyone who compels another Christian to tithe is sinning as much as those who compelled Christians to be circumcised.

So Christians should reject all exhortations to give based on Malachi 3 for three reasons. One, the quoting of Malachi 3 in the attempt to compel Christians to tithe is directly analogous to other practices expressly condemned in the New Testament, specifically the compulsion to undergo circumcision. Two, these exhortations are in direct conflict with 2 Corinthians 9:7, and three, these exhortations are completely inappropriate in Christianity given that the Law of the Old Testament, the undergirding authority of Malachi 3, has been canceled.

I think it is evident that there are two paradigms for Christian giving. One that is based on Old Testament texts like Malachi 3 and one that is based on New Testament texts like 2 Corinthians 9. I have witnessed both giving paradigms in operation on various occasions, and one day, I saw both in the same service. A common tenet of the modern-day tithe is that it is different than an offering. It is taught that tithes are required and offerings are free will. However, it is made clear that a gift cannot be considered an "offering" until the tithe has been paid in full. The tithe is the "first fruit" and is to be given before all other forms of giving. Offerings are only those gifts that are above and beyond the tithe.

Well, one day, a traveling evangelist came to the church I was attending. He was awesome. It was clear to everyone that this man was the real deal. He was humble yet spoke forcefully. He was a man who experienced tremendous pain in his life and had overcome many difficulties. He was robbed of nearly every form of human pride by a horrific event, and we knew that it could only be God that could have picked up the pieces of his life. Anyway, as is the custom at this church and many others, there was a collection taken up for his ministry. In fact, the evangelist made a specific request of us. He told us how he had acquired a literal "boatload" full of children's clothing from a major American manufacturer. These clothes had defects, so they couldn't be sold on the American market, but he wanted to take them over to Vietnam to give to underprivileged and in some cases literally naked children. He said the only obstacle to getting the clothes from the harbor in America to the children in Vietnam was the cost of shipping. So we gave him an offering which was above and beyond our tithes. When the pastor presented our gift to the evangelist, he made a few comments. To the best of my recollection, it went something like this,

"Mr. Evangelist, it is with great pleasure that we are able to give this gift. I always knew that this congregation was full of generous givers, but this gift even surpassed my expectations of what they would or even could do for you. To be honest, it's a little difficult to give this away. This gift is around twice as much as normal Sunday giving for this church. An amount like this sure would help us pay the bills around here. Obviously, we won't keep this gift to ourselves, but I encourage the church members to continue to give in the regular giving in this same manner..."

I was somewhat amused watching the pastor give this speech, because he did not know what to make of the situation. He was visibly troubled and confused. You could almost hear him think out loud, *Why aren't they this generous with regular giving?* Only God knows the real reason. Maybe it was due to the fact that a prophet is without honor in his hometown (and conversely, with great honor in a foreign town), but I have a different theory. The church I was attending believed strongly in the tithe. They had a special book that they would show to the congregation that contained the names of the tithers. The pastorship promised to pray for the people whose names were in the book. Every collection was preceded by an impassioned exhortation to give, usually with an explicit reference to the tithe. And it is my guess that people generally gave according to these expectations.

With regard to the traveling evangelist, my belief is that he made his request under the authority of the new law. As I remember it, he made his plea without a biblical reference and without making any promises of a blessing in return. He simply stated the need of the situation he was in. In doing this, he was operating in accordance with the law of the new covenant. And the people, refreshed by this, gave overwhelmingly. The people were free to give. And when you are free to give, you give with your heart. I believe that the people in that church have very sincere hearts and this evangelist tapped into the great reserve of love that was there. So even after the people had given what was "required" earlier in the service, they found a way to surpass that amount by nearly double during the "free will offering".

The point of this story is to illustrate the two ways in which Christian giving can be conducted (although I believe only one is truly Christian). There is the system of the Old Testament, which involves the tithe, or required giving. And let us be without pretense—it is based on compulsion. The alternative is the way of the new covenant, which involves giving according to the Spirit. My old church was choosing to implement a system of giving according to the old covenant. They reaped both the blessings and the curses of that covenant. The evangelist chose to ask for assistance according to the new covenant and was blessed correspondingly. If the church will abandon the tithe and embrace giving according to the Spirit, then I believe we will be revitalized as a body and we will be much more effective in our mission to the world.

7

Did Jesus Endorse the Tithe?

You should have practiced the latter
without leaving the former undone.

—Luke 11:42

Argument 5: Jesus himself endorsed the
tithe, and because it was a commandment of
Christ, if for no other reason, Christians
must tithe.

Did Jesus endorse the tithe? Did he say anything to suggest
that in the future, it would be paid to him? The English word
tithe does not appear in the New Testament in the NIV Bible,
but the tithe is referenced in three verses where Jesus speaks,

Woe to you, teachers of the Law and Pharisees, you hypocrites! You give a tenth of your spices—mint, dill, and cumin. But you have neglected the more important matters of the Law—justice, mercy, and faithfulness. You should have practiced the latter without neglecting the former. You blind guides! You strain out a gnat but swallow a camel. (Matt. 23:23–24)

Woe to you Pharisees, because you give God a tenth of your mint, rue and all other kinds of garden herbs, but you neglect justice and the love of God. You should have practiced the latter without leaving the former undone. (Luke 11:42)

"Two men went up to the temple to pray, one a Pharisee and the other a tax collector. The Pharisee stood up and prayed about himself: 'God, I thank you that I am not like other men—robbers, evildoers, adulterers—or even like this tax collector. I fast twice a week and give a tenth of all I get.'

But the tax collector stood at a distance. He would not even look up to heaven, but beat his breast and said, 'God, have mercy on me, a sinner.'

I tell you that this man, rather than the other, went home justified before God…" (Luke 18:10–14)

I have actually heard it said that this is Jesus's endorsement of the tithe. However, the purpose of these passages was to *condemn* the Pharisees and to say that the tithe is worthless without a commitment of the heart. Many of the modern-day tithe preachers would have you believe that tithing is how you demonstrate faithfulness. Matthew 23:23 says just the opposite: that it is possible to tithe without being faithful at all. Every time Jesus mentions the tithe, he does so in relation to the Pharisees. Because of this, it seems odd to me that this would qualify as the divine endorsement of a modern-day tithe. What we have to remember is that this statement was made when the Law still applied to the Jews. Everything changed after Jesus died, as was made clear in Hebrews (as we will see in the next section of this chapter). If Jesus was endorsing anything, it was that the tithe was binding on Jews at the time he made the statement (which was before his death). The fact that Jesus lumps the tithe in with "matters of the Law" is significant, I believe. I've spent a lot effort in this book trying to show you that the Law has been canceled. If the Law has been canceled and the tithe is part of the Law (as Jesus mentioned in the Gospels), then the tithe has been canceled.

There is yet one more argument that involves Jesus and tithing.

Argument 6: Jesus, as our High Priest, is due the tithe that has always been paid to God's priests. When the Law was changed from the old covenant law to the new covenant law, it meant that tithes are now due to Christ.

Some preachers of the tithe insist that Jesus, in his capacity as High Priest, now receives tithes. They point to Hebrews 7:12 as the basis for a Christian tithe, "For when there is a change of the priesthood, there must also be a change of the law" (Heb. 7:12).

They interpret this passage as meaning that tithing has always been in effect—first as pre-Law practice demonstrated by Abraham toward Melchizedek, next as a commandment of the Law in support of the Levites, and finally as a commandment to Christians (as a part of the new law) to give a tithe to Jesus.

The problem is, this idea is absent from the Bible. If we think again about the argument from silence, it is quite profound that an explicit reference to a tithe to Jesus is absent. It is only by the "argument from silence" that Hebrews 7:3 makes sense. We know Melchizedek was not immortal as Hebrews 7:3 would imply. The author is speaking from an ancient hard-line Jewish school of biblical interpretation to an audience that was familiar with this tradition. So let us consider again the passage of Scripture between Hebrews 7:3 and 7:12.

In Hebrews 7:3, the author clearly invokes the ancient tradition of interpretation which says that if something is not recorded in Scripture, then it did not happen. In Hebrews 7:5–10, the author talks about two tithes. These are the same two tithes (the Levitical tithe and Abraham's tithe) I discussed in chapters 3, 4, and 5. If you have believed me so far, we see that neither of these tithes is binding on Christians. There are teachers who say there is a third tithe established for Christians by Hebrews 7:12. The text obviously does not mention it explicitly, but these same people argue from inference that because the context of Hebrews 7:12 was the giving of tithes, what else could "a change of the law" be referring to?

I agree that the verse "a change of the law" would necessarily deal with the subject of the tithe. And I think we only have two options in interpreting Hebrews 7:12. The first option is that the "change of the law" was a change in who receives tithes, namely Jesus. The second option is that the "change of the law" was the canceling of the law and practice of tithing. Guess which interpretation I think is right?

Before I give my answer, read Hebrews 7:3–12 and think about the tradition of the argument from silence, priests and priesthoods, the two historical tithes, and the changing of the law.

> Without father or mother, without genealogy, without beginning of days or end of life, like the Son of God he [*Melchizedek*] remains a priest forever. [*by the argument from silence*]
>
> Just think how great he was: Even the patriarch Abraham gave him a tenth of the plunder! [*the first priest and the first tithe*] Now the law requires the descendants of Levi who become priests to collect a tenth from the people [*the second priesthood and the*

second tithe]—that is, their brothers—even though their brothers are descended from Abraham. This man, however, did not trace his descent from Levi, yet he collected a tenth from Abraham and blessed him who had the promises. And without doubt the lesser person is blessed by the greater. In the one case, the tenth is collected by men who die; but in the other case, by him [*Melchizedek, not Jesus*] who is declared to be living [*by the argument from silence*]. One might even say that Levi, who collects the tenth, paid the tenth through Abraham, because when Melchizedek met Abraham, Levi was still in the body of his ancestor.

If perfection could have been attained through the Levitical priesthood (for on the basis of it the law was given to the people), why was there still need for another priest to come—one in the order of Melchizedek, not in the order of Aaron? For when there is a change of the priesthood, there must also be a change of the law. (Heb. 7:3–12; emphases and commentary mine)

The very next line in scripture would be a perfect time to have a statement like, "This is why we tithe to Jesus, our high priest."

Wouldn't this flow rather well? But let's instead look at what Scripture does say:

He of whom these things are said belonged to a different tribe, and no one from that tribe has ever served at the altar. For it is clear that our Lord descended from Judah, and in regard to that tribe Moses said nothing about priests. And what we have said is even more clear if another priest like Melchizedek appears, one who has become a priest not on the basis of a regulation as to his ancestry but on the basis of the power of an indestructible life. For it is declared:

"You are a priest forever, in the order of Melchizedek." *The former regulation is set aside because it was weak and useless* (for the law made nothing perfect), and a better hope is introduced, by which we draw near to God. (Heb. 7:13–19; emphasis mine)

In my opinion, we had two options as to what the "change of the law" could mean. I think we now have two very good reasons to reject the idea that the author of Hebrews had in mind a Christian tithe. One, he doesn't explicitly mention it (i.e., the author was silent) in a portion of text in which he employed the argument from silence twice—Hebrews 7:3 and 7:8. Two, in Hebrews 7:18, he *does* explicitly say that "the former regulation is set aside." If the author was speaking of the entire law, why didn't he make reference to "regulations" (plural)? I'm asking this to make you think. It is my opinion he was speaking generically. It is my opinion that it would be an error in interpretation to say that the author of Hebrews had any one regulation in mind. I think what we have here is perhaps a peculiarity of the way he wrote. I think this because, to me, it is fairly clear he had the entire Mosaic law in mind. Hebrews 7:18 nullifies the entire Mosaic law. *But, what if* we were to nitpick the text for a single regulation that he was speaking of? What *one* regulation was the author talking about in Hebrews 7:4–10?

Tithing!

My friends, "the former regulation is set aside" means there is no Christian tithe! The "change of the law" was to abolish the tithe (because it was part of the old law), not to change the priest to whom it must be given.

Let's examine Hebrews for other scriptures which corroborate this. There is a great passage in Hebrews,

> Do not be carried away by all kinds of strange teachings. It is good for our hearts to be strengthened by grace, not by ceremonial foods, which are of no value to those who eat them. We have an altar from which those who minister at the tabernacle have no right to eat. (Heb. 13:9–10)

Let's examine this closely. What kind of "strange teachings" is the author talking about? He is talking about teachings which instruct Christians to go back to doing things the old Jewish way, especially tithing. Did the author really have tithing in mind? You decide. First he mentions that ceremonial foods "are of no value". Of course, in the old covenant, ceremonial foods did have value. But ceremonial foods don't have value for Christians. Then the author makes one the strongest criticisms of Judaism we will find in the New Testament in Hebrews 13:10. It is particularly telling, so I'm going to quote it again, "We have an altar from which those who minister at the tabernacle have no right to eat" (Heb. 13:10).

The context of this verse is ceremonial foods. It is saying that Christians eat from a different altar than whom? Who ministers at the tabernacle? The Levites. What were they ministers of? The old covenant. *What did they eat?* The tithe. Remember, the tithe was *food.*

> Be sure to set aside a tenth of all that your fields produce each year. Eat the tithe of your grain, new wine and oil, and the firstborn of your flocks in the presence of the Lord your God…(Deut. 14:22–23)

> Moreover, we will bring to the storerooms of the house of our God, to the priests, the first of our ground meal, of our grain offerings, of the fruit of all our trees and of our new wine and oil. And we will bring a tithe of our crops to the Levites, for it is the Levites who collect the tithes in all the towns where we work. (Neh. 10:37)

> Bring the whole tithe into the storehouse, that there may be food in my house. (Mal. 3:10)

In the old covenant, the Levites had the right to collect tithes and eat them in the presence of God. The author of Hebrews is contrasting the right of the old priesthood to eat sacred food in the presence of God with the Christian's right to eat in the presence of Jesus. From ancient times and continuing to this very day, there are people who believe that Christianity should be modeled after Judaism. I believe this is wrong, so I'm really going to pound this home. You absolutely must understand this truth, so I ask you (one more time) to read Hebrews 13:10.

> We have an altar from which those who minister at the tabernacle have *no right to eat.* (Heb. 13:10; emphasis mine)

Get this. *Those who eat the tithe have no right to dine with Jesus!* That's what this verse says. Why? The new has replaced the old, and they cannot commingle. You cannot pour new wine into old wineskins. When you think about the "sacred food" that Christians eat, you'll understand how profound Hebrews 13:10 is. What special, sacred, ritualistic, holy "food" do Christians eat? What food do Christians eat as part of their religion? Communion—the body and blood of Jesus. The communion table is the "altar" from which Christians eat. Hebrews 13:10 says that priests of the old covenant have no right to participate in Christian Communion. It's rather scary when you think about it: Christian pastors who presume to accept tithes are putting themselves in the same group of people who have "no right" to dine with Jesus. These same pastors are the ones putting forward "strange teachings" on tithing and Christian giving. I can only hope that someday they realize this.

Hopefully, now we can see how Hebrews 7 and 13 relate. In Hebrews 7, we understood that the former regulation of tithing (along with everything else in the Law) was set aside. We saw that when a new priesthood is established, a new law is also established. This new law completely supersedes (i.e., cancels and replaces) the old law. This is why Hebrews 13 talks about the old priests having no right to minister at the altar with the new priest. It is ridiculous to believe that the practices of the old priesthood now please the new priest.

In conclusion, we've looked at the sayings of Jesus in the Gospels and we've investigated the book Hebrews. Neither of these texts supports the idea of a Christian tithe. I hope I have shown that Jesus did not endorse tithing for his followers, nor did he ever expect to receive tithes from his followers. Lastly, I hope I have equipped you to see *why* Jesus would not want your tithe. And in the next chapter, we will see what Jesus *does* want from his followers.

Interlude 2

and a time to build

—Ecclesiastes 3:3

So we come to the end of the "negative" part of the book. My stated intention was to annihilate the notion that tithing is a binding commandment for Christians to follow. I presented many scriptures and much evidence against the classic arguments in favor of tithing. While these arguments came in various flavors and forms, I think the common thread throughout every argument is that something old (a command, a law, a precedent) is still valid today. The error behind all of these arguments is the idea that everything written in the Bible is somehow legally relevant (in the spiritual sense) for Christians. In my opinion, this error is analogous to arguing that drinking alcohol is immoral because it is forbidden by the Eighteenth Amendment of the US Constitution. As we all know, the Eighteenth Amendment was known as "Prohibition" and was repealed by the Twenty-First Amendment of the US Constitution. To extend the analogy, notice that the record of this law (the Eighteenth Amendment) was not stricken from the document. The Eighteenth Amendment is still very much a part of the Constitution, but it is not legally binding. That's because you must consider the entire document when deciding what is legal. When you survey the entire document, you find that the Twenty-First Amendment supersedes the Eighteenth Amendment. The Bible is very similar. The New

Testament would contradict the Old Testament if we did not have the proper understanding of the texts in the Old Testament. Similarly, if we did not understand the nature of the US Constitution, it would appear that the Eighteenth and Twenty-First Amendments contradict each other. When one law supersedes another, there is no contradiction. And this is precisely the situation we have between the Old and New Testaments.

Christians aptly call the Old Testament "old". Some people like to call the moral code of the Old Testament the "original covenant" or the "first covenant", using words implying that it is not out-of-date or obsolete. However, consider how strongly the New Testament labeled the old covenant: "By calling this covenant 'new,' he has made the first one obsolete, and what is obsolete and aging will soon disappear" (Heb. 8:13).

So the main error of the preachers of the tithe is a serious theological and doctrinal mistake. I know this sounds horribly condescending, but they do not realize how to properly interpret and apply scriptures from the Old Testament. I only say that because if an amateur like myself can figure this out, what excuse do these professionals have? In the natural, it would be easy to question the motive of the preachers of the tithe, given how obvious and strong the case against tithing is. Only God knows the motives of their hearts, so I'll leave that to Him. But, hopefully, you've been shown enough of the scriptures in both Testaments to recognize what is true and what is false.

But let's move on, shall we? I'm done arguing against the tithe. If tithing is not what we're supposed to do as Christians, then what are we to do? Ultimately, I'd rather be known for what I am for, not what I am against. The best material I've got is still yet to come. So please stay with me through the second half of this book.

8

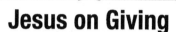

Jesus on Giving

Something Harder Than Tithing

Give to everyone who asks you, and if anyone takes
what belongs to you, do not demand it back.

—Matthew 6:30

So FAR, MOST of what has been written in this book has been
focused on what not to do. Now we turn our attention to the
positive, and ask the question, "How then are we as Christians
expected to give?" Of course, Jesus taught on giving and other
money matters. He made reference to money in many of his
parables. His teachings are brief and can be easily stated, but
like the rest of what he taught, his commandments turn out
to be even tougher than the old ones.

It is easy to see why the people were amazed at the authority with which Jesus preached. From the accounts that we have, he packed much truth into few words. His "Sermon on the Mount" is less than three pages long but has been the fodder for thousands of books and countless hours of conversations, lectures, sermons, and speeches. Everything he said and did was profound. His brevity was due to the fact that he brokered in the truth, and most of the time, the truth alone. What I mean by this is that in any field of human knowledge, the truth can be simply stated. For example, many mathematical textbooks condense all of their axioms and theorems on the insides of the cover. The mathematical truth of the whole book turns out to be very brief. What takes up space is explaining the truth, proving the truth, and applying the truth. It is my conjecture that Jesus, knowing his teaching career would be brief, did not spend much time in the explanation, proof, or application of the truth because he knew that we, as Christians, could work that out later. This is why the Holy Spirit is so vital in the life of the Christian. To fully understand the words of Jesus is a nontrivial task. What Jesus *said* is documented in the Gospels, but what Jesus *meant* can only be understood with the help of the Holy Spirit.

Naturally, Jesus did not have a lot to say about giving if we measure what was said according to its sheer volume. But what he said was potent and challenges our understanding to this day. He espoused a system of giving that was much harder to follow than the system in the Old Testament. In fact, there is probably no one in the world who has ever fully implemented his system of giving. In very practical terms, what he established is impossible to follow. But, then again, Jesus was never bothered by what we humans deem "practical" or "possible".

Let's examine what Jesus said about giving in the Sermon on the Mount,

> But I tell you who hear me: Love your enemies, do good to those who hate you, bless those who curse you, pray for those who mistreat you. If someone strikes you on the cheek, turn to him the other also. If someone takes your cloak, do not stop him from taking your tunic. *Give to everyone who asks you*, and if anyone takes what belongs to you, do not demand it back. Do to others what you would have them do to you.
>
> If you love those who love you, what credit is that to you? Even "sinners" love those who love them. And if you do good to those who do good to you, what credit is that to you? Even "sinners" do that. And if you lend to those from whom you expect repayment, what credit is that to you? Even "sinners" lend to "sinners," expecting to be repaid in full. But love your enemies, do good to them, and *lend to them without expecting to get anything back*. Then your reward will be great, and you will be called sons of the Most High, because He is kind to the ungrateful and wicked. (Luke 6:27–35; emphases added)

Jesus's instructions get pretty impossible pretty quick in the New Testament. This passage is not about giving per se, but we see how Jesus understood giving in the larger perspective of living a righteous life. I would be surprised if even one in a million Christians in America is living true to the command, "Give to everyone who asks you." Anyone who can live out this command has my utmost respect.

Another famous saying of Jesus on giving is in Matthew 22. The Pharisees came to Jesus to try and trap him into saying something that could get him in trouble. The Pharisees asked if it was right to pay taxes to Caesar. This was a yes-or-no question, and the Pharisees were prepared to attack him no matter what he said. If Jesus answered yes, then they would have attacked him as being sympathetic to the Romans and as a Jewish traitor—not holding to the promises of God concerning the land of Israel. If he answered no, then they would have reported him to the Romans as a lawbreaker and an instigator. Instead, he said, "Give to Caesar what is Caesar's, and give to God what is God's" (Matt. 22:21).

In this short statement, Jesus makes a couple of significant points. The first point is that secular taxes deserve to be paid. Jesus could have said a thousand bad things about Caesar and the Roman government at the time. He could have built a case justifying the Jews in withholding taxes to Rome. But since Caesar's face was on the very currency the Jews used to live, he condoned paying the Roman taxes. I believe he was saying that, "If you are going to participate in the Roman economy by using their currency for monetary transactions, then the Romans have the right to collect taxes on your income." I also believe that Jesus could have said, "Is it right to give as your tribute to God currency that is imprinted with the face of Caesar?" It is easy to see the irony in such a situation. With this in mind, I believe Jesus answered the Pharisees' question in the only consistent way that he could have. In the next chapter, we will see that Paul also addressed the subject of secular taxes. The second point that Jesus made is that there is giving that is due to God. The proponents of the modern-day tithe say that what is due to God is the tithe. Perhaps at the time when Jesus spoke those words, the tithe was due to God, but not anymore. In the parable of the Sheep and the Goats, Jesus defines what true giving to God is.

> "Then the King will say to those on his right, 'Come, you who are blessed by my Father; take your inheritance, the kingdom prepared for you since the creation of the world. For I was hungry and you gave me something to eat, I was thirsty and you gave me something to drink, I was a stranger and you invited me in, I needed clothes and you clothed me, I was sick and you looked after me, I was in prison and you came to visit me.' Then the righteous will answer him, 'Lord, when did we see you hungry and feed you, or thirsty and give you something to drink? When did we see you a stranger and invite you in, or needing clothes and clothe you? When did we see you sick or in prison and go visit you?' The King will reply, 'I tell you the

truth, whatever you did to the least of these brothers of mine, you did for me.'" (Matt. 25:34–40)

Giving to God, as He Himself defines it, is giving to the needy. This should not be too surprising, because it was a crucial element of the original system of giving in the Old Testament. But in the New Testament, Jesus equates it with giving to God directly. So when Jesus said, "Give to God what is God's," we know that at least part of what he had in mind was giving to the needy. In fact, when Jesus spoke about giving, he most frequently mentioned the poor.

> So when you give to the needy, do not announce it with trumpets, as the hypocrites do in the synagogues and on the streets, to be honored by men. I tell you the truth, they have received their reward in full. But when you give to the needy, do not let your left hand know what your right hand is doing, so that your giving may be done in secret. Then your Father, who sees what is done in secret, will reward you. (Matt. 6:2–4)

> If you want to be perfect, go, sell your possessions and give to the poor, and you will have treasure in heaven. Then come, follow me. (Matt. 19:21; also Mark 10:21 and Luke 18:22)

> Sell your possessions and give to the poor. Provide purses for yourselves that will not wear out, a treasure in heaven that will not be exhausted, where no thief comes near and no moth destroys. (Luke 12:33)

When you give a luncheon or dinner, do not invite your friends, your brothers or relatives, or your rich neighbors; if you do, they may invite you back and so you will be repaid. But when you give a banquet, invite the poor, the crippled, the lame, the blind, and you will be blessed. Although they cannot repay you, you will be repaid at the resurrection of the righteous. (Luke 14:12–13)

Your prayers and gifts to the poor have come up as a memorial offering before God. (Acts 10:4; an angel speaking for Christ)

Jesus's emphasis on the poor is important. The tithe, of course, was mandatory for all of Israel (except for the poor obviously), and the poor were rightful beneficiaries of the tithe. Jesus did not explicitly state that giving to the poor was mandatory, but Jesus emphasized no other group so strongly in terms of giving while he was on earth. Now the modern-day proponents of the tithe will tell you it is still mandatory, but they totally neglect the aspect of the tithe that was devoted to the poor. They will tell you that tithing is "giving to God", but they largely ignore the teaching of Jesus that giving to the poor is "giving to God". Regardless of any notion of the tithe, or required giving, it is clear that every believer in Christ should be a devoted giver to the poor.

Jesus also addressed giving to God through giving to one's family. Again, the Pharisees were the ones who prompted Jesus to say.

"And why do you break the command of God for the sake of your tradition? For God said, 'Honor you father and mother' and 'Anyone who curses his father or mother must be put to death.' But you say that if a man says to his father or mother, 'Whatever help you might have received from me is a gift devoted to God,' he is not to 'honor' his father with it. Thus you nullify the word of God for the sake of your tradition..." (Matt. 15:3–6)

I believe the point to be learned from this passage is that charity among family is not to be at the mercy of charity outside the family, even if that means withholding gifts to your church. Jesus demonstrates that there is a hierarchy of commandments: some are more important than others. How can we know which ones are the most important? Two ways: by the revelation of the Holy Spirit and by love. The tithe, or gifts "devoted to God", was *mandatory* for the Jews. As we saw in the previous chapter, Jesus condoned tithing for the Jews while the Law was in effect. But, then, Jesus said in Matthew 15 that if there is tension between two commandments of God, then the one to be observed is the one motivated by love. Jesus implied that your love for your family must exceed your love of the church, which should not be confused with your love for God. One can express love for God in many ways, two of which are love for the family and love for the church. Even though God desires gifts made to the church, He would much rather have you take care of your immediate family first. This flies in the face of one of the common tenets of the modern-day tithe. Some modern-day Pharisees proclaim that there are no exceptions—the tithe is the Lord's (meaning the church's) always. Obviously, this notion fails the test of Scripture. Even when the tithe was still in effect, Jesus condemned this hard-line position. Love is greater than service, sacrifice, or duty, and we should always be motivated by love when deciding how to give.

So much of what is preached today is based on giving to God what is God's. When Jesus came, he told the Jews that their idea of giving to God was mistaken and had become contaminated with the ideas of men. Unfortunately, by preaching the tithe, some modern pastors have still not learned the essence of Christ's message concerning giving to God.

Is there anything that Jesus said concerning giving to a Christian church? The short answer is no. He did, however, claim that his disciples deserved to be provided for by the people they served. When Jesus sent the seventy-two disciples out two by two, he gave them these instructions:

> "Go! I am sending you out like lambs among wolves. Do not take a purse or bag or sandals; and do not greet anyone on the road.
>
> When you enter a house, first say, 'Peace to this house.' If a man of peace is there, your peace will rest on him; if not, it will return to you. Stay in that house eating and drinking whatever they give you, for the worker deserves his wages." (Luke 10:5–7)

Jesus gave similar instructions to the twelve disciples when he sent them out (Matt. 10:10). Jesus established that messengers of the Gospel have the right to support from the recipients of the Gospel. This teaching applies to the present-day local church. But other than this instruction, Jesus said very little that could be applied specifically to today's local church.

Even though Jesus was quiet concerning giving to the local church, this matter is important and will be addressed in a later chapter. But I do believe Jesus taught the way in which a pastor should ask for money. Jesus said regarding oaths, "Simply let your 'Yes' be 'Yes', and your 'No' be 'No'; anything beyond this comes from the evil one…" (Matt. 5:37).

By analogy, I believe that pastors should simply ask for the money they need. I tell you that the tendency to add anything to a simple request for money is an impulse from Satan. In my opinion, based on Matthew 5:37, pastors should humbly make the needs of the church known to the congregation and should simply ask for the money to meet these needs. In response, the congregation should give to the church what it needs according to the request. If we as Christians are commanded by Jesus to give our enemies what they ask of us, how much more are we expected to give to those we love who ask of us! The hallmark of the church is supposed to be love. When the pastor addresses the church, it should be as if he is among family. He should know and love his flock, and they should know and love him. So when he asks for money, he should receive it as if his own family were helping him. This is how I believe it should be in Christianity today. I was very impressed by a traveling evangelist who asked for money in this way: he said, "If I have helped you and if you think my message is worth spreading, I ask you to please support my ministry." I believe he was acting in accordance with the will of our loving Savior.

Concerning how children of God were to be provided for, Jesus said,

> "So do not worry, saying, 'What shall we eat?', or 'What shall we drink?', or 'What shall we wear?' For the pagans run after all these things, and your heavenly Father knows that you need them. But seek first His Kingdom and His righteousness, and all these things will be given to you as well." (Matt. 6:31–32)

If pastors are truly seeking first the Kingdom of God, God Himself promises to provide for them. However, modern pastors seem to be saying one thing and doing another. Modern Christian leaders assert: "The tithe isn't about money. It's about putting God first in your life." But is tithing really putting God first? We are constantly told to "trust God" with our money and our financial giving, but it is obvious that Christian leaders do not trust God! If they really trusted God, they wouldn't engage in these manipulative tactics to get people to give.

For Jesus also said,

> Ask and it will be given to you; seek and you will
> find; knock and the door will be opened for you. For
> everyone who asks receives; he who seeks finds; and
> to him who knocks, the door will be opened. (Matt.
> 7:7–8)

Of course, these promises are for all Christians. *So why don't our leaders just ask?* Why all the extra stuff? Stuff like "Give in faith", "Trust God", "Put God first", "Don't rob from God", "Give and you shall receive", "God loves a cheerful giver", and on and on. By hammering these slogans into our heads, our Christian leaders demonstrate their own lack of faith that God does in fact provide!

Finally, one of the most significant statements Jesus made concerning giving was made without saying anything. While Jesus was in front of perhaps his largest crowd ever, he did something that I believe should never be forgotten. He *gave* to the people, not the other way around. The ministry of Jesus did not happen for free, and I think we can infer that there were financiers of his ministry. But Jesus never asked the people he ministered to for money. Even though he taught that God's messengers have the right to the support of the people, he did not use this right. In fact, when he fed the thousands, he established an important precedent. Those truly conducting the work of God will be provided for supernaturally. Since Jesus was truly "seeking first the kingdom of God", all of his needs were met, and they were met in such abundance that he could feed thousands of others and had enough for leftovers. We also see this principle in effect when Jesus paid his and Peter's temple tax with a coin that was in the mouth of a fish Peter caught. Jesus was miraculously provided for over and over again. I believe modern Christian leaders would do well to remember this. Those who prod and implore and coerce and exhort their audiences to give are doing something Jesus never had to.

9

Paul on Giving

Practical Advice

Anyone who receives instruction in the word
must share all good things with his instructor.

—Galatians 6:6

IN MY OPINION, Paul is the most relevant and authoritative
voice in the New Testament for Christians today. I will even
go as far to say that the words of Paul are even more applicable
than the words of Jesus. Right away, some of you may be
thinking that I am going too far. Please understand what I am
saying. Is Paul greater than Jesus? Of course not! Are Paul's
words any more truthful than the words of Jesus? Absolutely
not! Is there any conflict between the words of Jesus and

those of Paul? No! In fact, Paul was Jesus's mouthpiece after the Lord's ascension. In fact, one might say that Jesus was speaking directly through Paul and thus eliminate any tension between the two voices recorded in the New Testament.

The reason I believe that the words of Paul are so important is that he wrote for the purpose of providing clear instruction. Jesus spoke in riddles and parables, and only some of them are explained in the text. Jesus was intentionally cryptic when he spoke in order to fulfill prophecy. Jesus spoke to Jews, meaning (in many cases) that his message was in the context of the covenant which bound the Jews. His audience included those he despised, namely the religious leaders of his day. Of even greater significance when considering the words of Jesus is that he spoke when the Law was still in effect. The very essence of human reality changed after Jesus was crucified, but we have very few words of Jesus after his resurrection. By contrast, Paul usually did not teach Jews; he wrote to specific Gentile Christian churches. Paul expounded the truths of the new covenant and the new law which accompanied it. All of his teaching was based on God's truth for a new era (the church age), which was (and is) radically different than the era of the Mosaic law. Therefore, for matters of church practice, we should esteem the writings of Paul first and foremost because

1. He wrote in order to be understood
2. He wrote specifically to believers
3. He wrote based on the truths of the new covenant

So now we will study Paul's teachings.

Naturally, Paul addressed the subject of Christian giving. We have already been exposed to several of Paul's teachings in the first half of this book. Having covered these parts of the New Testament already, let us examine other teachings of Paul on giving. Appropriately, Paul continued many of the themes that Jesus introduced. Jesus said, "Give to Caesar what is Caesar's, and give to God what is God's." Paul carried this idea even further as it applies to Christians:

> Everyone must submit himself to the governing authorities, for there is no authority except that which God has established. The authorities that exist have been established by God. Consequently, he who rebels against the authority is rebelling against what God has instituted, and those who do so bring judgment on themselves. For rulers hold no terror for those who do right, but for those who do wrong. Do you want to be free from fear of the one in authority? Then do what is right and he will commend you. For he is God's servant to do you good. But if you do wrong, be afraid, for he does not bear the sword for nothing. He is God's servant, an agent of wrath to bring punishment on the wrongdoer. Therefore it is necessary to submit to the authorities, not only because of possible punishment but also because of conscience. This is why you pay taxes, for the authorities are God's servants, who give their full time to governing. Give everyone what you owe him: if you owe taxes, pay taxes; if revenue, then

revenue; if respect, then respect; if honor, then honor.
(Rom. 13:1–8)

Paul makes perfectly clear what Jesus meant. Jesus made a pithy statement in response to a challenge. Paul expounded the profound truth contained within that statement. According to Paul, the secular government is an agency of God, and therefore, it is necessary to give them money. For the modern Christian, the act of paying taxes honestly is a tribute to God in both senses of the word. The first sense of the word *tribute* is that of a testimony. The second sense of the word is that of a payment in acknowledgment of submission and/or protection. Paying taxes honestly can be a testimony to the character of God as well as a payment in acknowledgment of the divine sovereignty of the government. So according to Paul, you can give what is due Caesar and what is due God *at the same time.*

Paul also continued Jesus's teaching that charity begins at home.

> Give proper recognition to those widows who really are in need. But if a widow has children or grandchildren, these should learn first of all to put their religion into practice by caring for their own family and so repaying their parents and grandparents, for this is pleasing to God. The widow who is really in need and left all alone puts her hope in God and continues night and day to pray and to ask God for

> help…Give the people these instructions, too, so that
> no one may be open to blame. If anyone does not
> provide for his relatives, and especially his immediate
> family, he has denied the faith and is worse than an
> unbeliever. (1 Tim. 5:3–5,7–8)

Here again, Paul applies a teaching of Jesus in a very practical way for us in the church.

Paul resumed Jesus's themes on giving to messengers of the Gospel. And like Christ, whom he imitated, the life of Paul itself is a lesson in giving. It appears that Paul believed he was due financial support from the Gentile churches he served. Please read all of 1 Corinthians 9, but I want to draw your attention specifically to these verses:

> Who serves as a soldier at his own expense? Who
> plants a vineyard and does not eat of its grapes? Who
> tends a flock and does not drink of the milk? Do I say
> this merely from a human point of view? Doesn't the
> Law say the same thing? For it is written in the Law
> of Moses: (1 Cor. 9:7–9)

Stop! I want you to think about two things. First, why is Paul appealing to the law of Moses when he himself was the primary person responsible for telling us it was canceled? Second, what verses from the law of Moses would a modern preacher quote to justify that his flock support him? Okay, now back to Paul.

"Do not muzzle an ox while it is treading out the grain." Is it about oxen that God is concerned? Surely he says this for us, doesn't he? Yes, this was written for us, because when the plowman plows and the thresher threshes, they ought to do so in the hope of sharing in the harvest. If we have sown spiritual seed among you, is it too much if we reap a material harvest from you? If others have this right of support from you, shouldn't we have it all the more? (1 Cor. 9:9–12)

We see in this passage that Paul claims to have the right to financial support for his spiritual service. But why is his biblical reference to oxen? He makes this rather bizarre reference not once but twice in the New Testament: "For the Scripture says, 'Do not muzzle the ox while it is treading out the grain,' and 'The worker deserves his wages'" (1 Tim. 5:18).

In reference to the first question I asked, let's try to reason why Paul (of all people) would base anything on the old law. It is very interesting to me that he references the old law as it applies to animals and not people. Paul, more than anyone, taught that the Law had been canceled for people. I think Paul is really appealing here to the idea that God is fair more than he is appealing to the authority of the old law. Paul was not quoting the old law as an authoritative moral code. He was using the Law as a history lesson on the character of God. If I may paraphrase Paul, I think he was saying, "If God (at any point in history) bothered to tell us to be fair to oxen who work for us, how much more would he tell us to be fair to people!" I'll leave it at that for now, because I have much more to say about this later.

In reference to the second question I posed, "How many times has your pastor told you that you should give to the church because oxen shouldn't be muzzled while treading the grain?" I have not heard any pastor use this verse. How about you? Pastors that I've heard use passages like Malachi 3. This is odd (isn't it?), because Paul is directly addressing the support of a Christian ministry. You would think that a modern pastor would justify his own support on the same thing Paul based his support, especially if the modern pastor is building a scriptural basis for his support. I mean, it's not like the ancient Christians didn't have the same issues we do. We see right here in 1 Corinthians that Paul needed money for his ministry. We have the exact same situation today. So why aren't the ministers today preaching what Paul preached? Anyway...

The precedent of Paul using oxen to justify the support of his ministry is interesting. I say this because there were plenty of places in the old law which told us how to treat people in spiritual service to God, namely the priests. Why does Paul appeal to the more general principle of fairness instead of the rights of the priests? Paul was well aware of the rights of priests and Levites to receive the support of the people they served. In 1 Corinthians 9:13–14, Paul states very clearly the similarity between his ministry and the ministry of the Levites.

Pay close attention to what Paul is saying in these verses:

> Don't you know that those who work in the temple get their food from the temple, and those who serve at the altar share in what is offered at the altar? *In the same way* the Lord has commanded that those who preach the gospel should receive their living from the gospel. (1 Cor. 9:13–14; emphasis mine)

Stop! Wait a minute! Let's examine this phrase "in the same way". Paul is referencing old covenant practices again. This time, he isn't talking about oxen. He is comparing his ministry to the ministry of the priests and Levites. He said that Christian ministers should be supported "in the same way" as old covenant priests and Levites. The old covenant priests and Levites were supported by tithes and offerings. Does this mean that we have found proof that the tithe should be paid to Christian pastors? I do not think so. Again, as with Hebrews 7:12, we have a choice between two options. The phrase "in the same way" could be referring to the way of tithes and offerings, or it could be referring to something else. When you consider how much material we have already covered, I really believe Paul was talking about something other than tithes. First of all, yet again, we have a situation where we would have to read that interpretation (tithing) into the text, because an explicit mention of tithing is absent. If Paul had really meant to suggest that the Corinthians were neglectful in paying tithes, why did he not explicitly tell them so? He had every opportunity when he quoted the

Law in verse 9:9 to bring up the tithe. But he did not. And by now, I think we have a really good understanding why Paul was so careful to avoid the mention of the tithe. Paul would have undermined his entire message of freedom in Christ and his message of life in the Spirit if he would have endorsed the tithe or mandated that churches give to him. Elsewhere in his writings (Romans, Galatians, and Hebrews), he totally dismantled the old covenant, the old law, and the old priesthood. He could not possibly have extended the tithe given his other writings; it would have been completely inconsistent with the rest of his theology. Think about it!

So what does Paul mean that he deserves to be supported "in the same way" as priests?

If I may call your attention back to an argument I made in chapter 2, you may remember that I made the claim that the tithe (properly interpreted from Scripture) was a mathematically *fair* compensation for the priests and Levites. What was the fair amount that was due to the Levites? According to my calculations in chapter 2 of this book, the fair amount would have been approximately 3 percent of each individual's income. This amount is very close to the percentage associated with the tithe due to the Levites as it is interpreted from a straightforward reading of the Torah. What is the fair amount in Christianity? It is not fixed. It may not be 10 percent. It depends on the situation. But the principle of fairness applies, as well as the principle of love. And the essence of these principles is this: *give to those who help you spiritually.* *This* is the precedent set by Abraham in giving to Melchizedek, *not the tenth*. Melchizedek blessed Abraham, and then Abraham gave to him according to the principle of fairness. This is the essence of what Paul is saying here. Again, if I may paraphrase Paul, he is saying, "I deserve to be supported because it is fair. God has always been concerned about his workers receiving their fair share—whether it be Melchizedek, or Levitical priests, or even the oxen which work for his people, and me too!"

Even if you believe Paul was arguing that he had the right to be paid tithes (which I vehemently disagree with), let's look again at 1 Corinthians 9 to see what Paul did with this right.

> But I have not used any of these rights. And I am not writing this in the hope that you will do such things for me. I would rather die than have anyone deprive me of this boast. Yet when I preach the gospel, I cannot boast, for I am compelled to preach. Woe to me if I do not preach the gospel! If I preach voluntarily, I have a reward; if not voluntarily, I am simply discharging the trust committed to me. What then is my reward? Just this: that in preaching the gospel I may offer it free of charge, and so not make use of my rights in preaching it. (1 Cor. 9:15–18)

This "right" Paul was talking about was his right to be supported fairly, not the "right" to be paid tithes. But beyond this, we see a very important principle: the Gospel should be preached voluntarily and free of charge! That's the whole point of this book! Everything in Christianity should be "free to give". We should be free to give our money. We should be free to give our love and our service to others, and we should give instruction freely to others. This is the legacy of Christ and his appointed apostle Paul. I'm trying to follow their example, and I'm trying to get you (my audience) to do the same. I tell you it is the only way go!

The tendency of Paul to put the needs of his flock above his own is not an isolated or sparse element of his epistles. We see this theme again in his letters to the Thessalonians.

> As apostles of Christ we could have been a burden to you, but we were gentle among you, like a mother caring for her little children. We loved you so much that we were delighted to share with you not only the gospel of God but our lives as well, because you had become so dear to us. Surely you remember, brothers, our toil and hardship; we worked night and day in order not to be a burden to anyone while we preached the Gospel of God to you. (1 Thess. 2:6b–9)

And again...

> In the name of the Lord Jesus Christ, we command you, brothers, to keep away from every brother who is idle and does not live according to the teaching you received from us. For you yourselves know how you ought to follow our example. We were not idle when we were with you, nor did we eat

anyone's food without paying for it. On the contrary, we worked night and day, laboring and toiling so that we would not be a burden to any of you. We did this, not because we do not have the right to such help, but in order to make ourselves a model for you to follow. (2 Thess. 3:6–9)

By conducting himself in this way, Paul was living out the example set by Jesus. In the previous chapter, we saw the precedent Jesus set by giving to those he ministered to. Jesus laid no claim to the possessions of others, preferring to take on the role of servant and to help meet the earthly needs of the people he served. Likewise, Paul, being a God-ordained apostle to the Gentiles, had the right to receive money from everyone he served. But Paul set aside this right whenever he thought that those he served would be hindered or burdened by such a demand. By his own words, Paul was living out "a model for you to follow." We might ask, "Who is 'you'?" "You" is *us*! We are supposed to live like this. If anyone's ministry cannot survive without a constant reminder for support, then maybe the ministry is not from God and does not deserve to persist. I tell you, as a messenger of God to the Church, if Christian service in ministry is not voluntary and if the Christian support of that ministry is not also voluntary, then something is not right.

Don't believe for one second that I think we should not give to Christian ministries. Don't read this book and think I'm saying that all preachers should have to work a secular job on top of being a pastor. Don't misconstrue my words to mean that pastors should never have to ask for money. If you take anything away from this book, take this: the most important aspect of the existence of any Christian ministry (in terms of money) is that its support is derived from truly free-will gifts.

Since this chapter is subtitled "Practical Advice", I will conclude with three exhortations from Paul concerning giving.

> Now about the collection for God's people: Do what I told the Galatian churches to do. On the first day of every week each one of you should set aside a sum of money in keeping with his income, saving it up, so that no collections will have to be made. (1 Cor. 16:1–2)

We can see the consistent theme of Paul's writings on giving. Paul exhorts the Corinthians to set aside a fair amount, voluntarily, to be given away to others in need.

Next is a passage from 2 Corinthians.

> Our desire is not that others might be relieved while you are hard-pressed, but that there might be equality. At the present time your plenty will supply what they need, so that in turn their plenty will supply what you need. Then there will be equality, as it is written: "He who gathered much did not have too much, and he who gathered little did not have too little." (2 Cor. 8:13–15)

The pattern and commandment of Christian giving are clear. Give your fair share to those in need and to those who help you spiritually.

The final passage comes from 1 Timothy and is not expressly about giving, but it has do with money and it represents yet another instance in which Paul restates a fundamental truth first taught by Jesus.

> Command those who are rich in the present world not to be arrogant nor put hope in their wealth, which is so uncertain, but to put their hope in God, who richly provides us with everything for our enjoyment. Command them to do good, to be rich in good deeds, and to be generous and willing to share. In this way they will lay up treasure for themselves as a firm foundation for the coming age, so that they may take hold of the life that is truly life. (1 Tim. 6:17–19)

Here Paul states two commands for the wealthy. As is his hallmark, Paul uses words like "generous" and "share" when it comes to money practices. I believe that these verses apply to just about every American. We are so blessed, and we are so wealthy when you consider the rest of the world. I think we would all do well to remember "the life that is truly life" when conducting our financial affairs. Let us use our wealth and our freedom to give surpassingly, from a heart that loves overwhelmingly, and thus fulfill the call from God to the church.

10

The Paradox of the Two Principles
of Christian Giving

> Whoever finds his life will lose it, and whoever
> loses his life for my sake will find it.
>
> —Matthew 10:39

IN THE PAST two chapters, we have seen that while the endorsement of the tithe is absent from the New Testament, the subject of giving is everywhere. Both Jesus and Paul, not to mention the other writers, had much to say about giving. In this chapter, we will explore a powerful synthesis of the truths taught by Paul and Jesus. This synthesis of ideas results in two principles which should guide Christian giving. In fact, I tell you these two principles are fundamental laws of spiritual reality that indeed govern Christian giving in the same way that the law of gravity governs motion. Jesus revealed the first principle of Christian giving, and it is this: you reap what you sow. This is true in all areas of life, but especially for giving. Some call this the "law of the harvest". Jesus illustrated this principle by saying,

> Give, and it will be given to you. A good measure, pressed down, shaken together, running over, will be poured into your lap. For with the measure you use, it will be measured to you. (Luke 6:38)

Paul reemphasized this principle in one of his letters to the Corinthians:

> Remember this: Whoever sows sparingly will also reap sparingly, and whoever sows generously will also reap generously. Each man should give what he has decided in his heart to give, not reluctantly or under compulsion, for God loves a cheerful giver. And God is able to make all grace abound to you, so that in all things at all times, having all that you need, you will abound in every good work. (2 Cor. 9:6–8)

Unfortunately, there are many who teach this principle of giving without teaching its conjugate. This second principle is critically important in applying the first principle to the matter of giving. Although Jesus does not explicitly state the second principle, it is inherent in several of his teachings.

Paul, on the other hand, does explicitly state the principle. This second principle comes from arguably the most well-known passage in the New Testament: the love chapter, "If I give all I have to the poor and surrender my body to the flames, but have not love, I gain nothing" (1 Cor. 13:3).

We have already learned that giving to the poor is giving to God Himself. Giving to the poor pleases God. But in this passage, Paul negates giving in any manner that is not motivated by love. This truth was discernible in the teachings of Jesus as well. It just was not stated so directly (remember Matt. 6:1–4 and Luke 14:12–13).

The problem with taking the first principle in isolation is that it suggests that all giving benefits the giver. Paul says that there are circumstances in which the giver will "gain nothing". But taking these two principles in union implies that it is of the utmost importance that one's motives be immaculately pure in the matter of giving. This means that the whole issue of Christian giving is subordinate to something more fundamental. The primary issue here is one of character. The act of giving does not make one righteous. Giving can occur for many reasons, and I tell you that righteousness precedes righteous giving. First, we must die to the world. Then we must become totally selfless. Only when we give no thought to the reciprocation of a gift does the gift get credited to our account (remember Luke 6:32–35).

Paul's words presented earlier now especially ring true, "For if the willingness is there, the gift is acceptable according to what one has, not according to what he does not have" (2 Cor. 8:12).

What if Paul had been speaking of the love in our hearts as being the thing that is acceptable? From this text, in conjunction with the others presented, I think we can infer that a gift is only acceptable to the extent that it is given in love. In this context, we can perhaps more fully appreciate Jesus's statement to the Pharisees,

> Now then, you Pharisees clean the outside of the cup and dish, but inside you are full of greed and wickedness. You foolish people! Did not the one who made the outside make the inside also? But give what is inside the dish to the poor, and everything will be clean for you. (Luke 11:39–41)

I think we really need to read between the lines here. Jesus acknowledged that on the surface, the Pharisees were doing the right things, including giving to the poor. In essence, the Pharisees were giving to the poor from the "outside of the cup". They gave in order to be seen. They gave because they were required to by the Law. They gave because they thought it would make them righteous in the sight of God. They gave because they wanted God to bless them. But their giving was not credited to them in any way by Jesus. Instead, when Jesus said, "Give what is inside the dish to the poor", he was commanding them to love the poor. *Then* their gifts would be acceptable, and they would be "clean" in every way.

The truth is that you can be forced to give, but you cannot be forced to love. This isn't just ten times harder than tithing. It is infinitely harder than tithing. Some say that withholding the tithe is robbing from God, but the people who are truly robbing God are those who withhold their hearts from Him. Even in the Old Testament, when giving was required by the Law, God said, "For I desire mercy, not sacrifice, and acknowledgment of God rather than burnt offering" (Hosea 6:6).

Jesus reemphasized this aspect of God in his teaching (Matt. 9:13, 12:7). God has always desired the things of the heart, the things "inside the cup", above any external demonstration based on regulations.

Unfortunately, we have lost sight of this original message. So much attention is paid to the act of giving, and to sacrifice, and to the tithe, when the more fundamental issue is love. This is why Paul condemns giving under compulsion. It is worthless. Again, it is my firm conviction that the body of Christ should abandon the tithe, if for no other reason than it is not based in love.

Sadly, the law of the harvest has been exalted above all other principles of giving. The principle has been corrupted by the selfish ambition of man and in its corrupted form, is marked by the phrases *giving in faith* or *sowing in faith*. These ideas are always characterized as "biblical" by the ones espousing them, except they are inconsistent with the rest of the New Testament. What I think is really meant by these terms is "give more than you should and have faith that God will make it up to you" or "give and have faith that God will give it back." Haven't we all been exposed, in one way or another, to the statement, "You're still having problems in the area of your finances because you haven't learned to give in faith"? Honestly, what is the "faith" for? Faith is defined for us in Hebrews, "Now faith is being sure of what we hope for and certain of what we do not see" (Heb. 11:1).

So in the matter of giving, what is it that is hoped for and what is not seen? Truth be told, it is the blessing that you are going to get in return. This is the implicit, if not completely outright, message of those preaching "giving in faith". Actually, "giving in faith" really means giving in greed, because the "faith" is for the purpose of getting something back in return. However, the clarion call of the New Testament is to give in love. First Corinthians 13 subordinates *everything* to love. Nothing whatsoever matters or is credited as righteousness if it is not done in love. God isn't looking for people to bargain with Him; He's looking for those pure in heart.

Jesus repeatedly warned against giving out of selfish motives. Of course, "giving in faith" is never called being "selfish", but the best lies are the subtle ones. Consider the words of Christ again:

> When you give a luncheon or dinner, do not invite your friends, your brothers or relatives, or your rich neighbors; if you do, they may invite you back and so you will be repaid. But when you give a banquet, invite the poor, the crippled, the lame, the blind, and

you will be blessed. Although they cannot repay you,
you will be repaid at the resurrection of the righteous.
(Luke 14:12–13)

If Jesus says not to give to people who can repay, we
certainly should not give "expecting in faith" that God will
repay us. Please understand, the first principle guarantees that
we will be repaid, but our motivation and expectation should
not be that we will be repaid. If we give out of the wrong
motives, our repayment is canceled by the second principle.
This truth is paradoxical, much like what Jesus taught
concerning life itself, "Whoever tries to keep his life will lose
it, and whoever loses his life will preserve it" (Luke 17:33).

I tell you that whoever gives a gift expecting anything in
return from God or man will receive nothing and whoever
gives a gift expecting nothing in return will be repaid in this
life and the life to come. This is the way of the new covenant.
The only way that "giving in faith" works is to participate in
the old covenant, continuing in the practice established by
Jacob which was mentioned in chapter 5.

I have heard many testimonies about how tithing, or
"giving in faith", has blessed the giver. Well, the old covenant
is not without blessing, but I believe another principle is at
work in the lives of these blessed givers. God honors faith
and obedience, and in his mercy, he blesses the ignorant
but devoted giver. I've experienced this in my own life. As a
teenager, I was inspired by Robert Tilton to "make a vow and

pay it" (Ps. 50) as a means to blessing. I gave away the only college scholarship I had, worth $1,000. In my ignorance (of both Robert Tilton's character and the truth of Scripture: don't even make a vow at all—Matthew 5:34), I relied on God to meet my financial needs for college. But what I was really doing was giving to get back. I was blessed within two weeks of making my vow with over $13,000 in scholarships for my freshman year alone, more than the cost of attending college. Before I had given Mr. Tilton the entire pledge, he was exposed on the TV show *20/20* as a charlatan. I repented before God for my ignorance and lack of discernment, and I gave the rest of the money I vowed to my local church. What I didn't realize until years later was that I was turning my back on the new covenant by embracing the promises of financial blessing of the old. I now realize that the promises, blessings, and curses of the Old Testament come as a package deal, and life with Christ is much better. I believe that God forgave me and had mercy on me, and continues to do so, for my participation in ignorance in the old covenant because He knows what I really want is to be part of the new covenant.

True new covenant giving is patently different. The very nature of God confirms what true giving is. God gave something to us, in the form of His Son, that is impossible to repay: forgiveness of our sins. He also gives us eternal life. What can we possibly give to God in return for this? Nothing. And this is precisely the attitude He wants us to have. Jesus said, "Freely you have received, freely give" (Matt. 10:8).

To give "freely" means to give without any expectations placed on the gift. Free giving means to totally release the gift to the recipient. It is in this light that I believe Jesus spoke the words, "I do not give to you as the world gives" (John 14:37).

This is one of the most profound truths of our faith. I exhort my audience to pause and reflect on what this means. In particular, think about how the world gives. What would happen if you walked up to a complete stranger and gave him $100? You can almost hear what he would say, *What's the catch?* No one of this world ever gives anything for free—there is always a *catch*, isn't there? Jesus has given to us freely, and true Christianity is manifested in us giving in the image, or example, of Christ. I'm telling you that Jesus would appreciate it if we gave back to him without a catch. But that would mean we would have to drop this whole idea of "giving in faith".

So when Jesus spoke of laying up treasure in heaven, he was actually speaking of something very difficult to do.

> Do not store up for yourselves treasures on earth, where moth and rust destroy, and where thieves break in and steal. But store up for yourselves treasures in heaven, where moth and rust do not destroy, and where thieves do not break in and steal. (Matt. 6:19–20)

Considering the second principle of Christian giving, this is nearly impossible, because we cannot seek to store up treasure for ourselves. If treasure is what we seek, then we will lose it. Your heart goes to heaven first, then your treasure. If you have been duped by the "giving in faith" message, you are not even seeking treasure in heaven but treasure on earth. Consider the $1,000 I gave away as a teenager. I am sure that not one penny has been imputed to me as righteousness. Perhaps my faith was credited to me, but I received that credit in the here and now. Not one cent of the original $1,000 has been laid up in heaven. I have been paid in full. Giving to receive something on earth is especially dangerous given what Jesus taught in the very same lesson.

> No one can serve two masters. Either he will hate the one and love the other, or he will be devoted to the one and despise the other. You cannot serve both God and Money. (Matt. 6:24)

Therefore, I believe giving cannot serve dual purposes. You either give a gift expecting something in return, or you completely release it. If you give "expectantly", then you may receive an earthly blessing as I did, but the eternal blessing has been, in essence, "cashed out". But if you truly release the gift, it will be waiting for you in heaven.

Having written all of this, "giving in faith", in my opinion, is just as detestable to God as the worn-out notion of the tithe. God promises to meet our needs without us having to bargain with him (Matt. 6, Luke 12). So let us once and for all dismiss the notion of giving to get back, no matter what language this heresy is couched in.

In conclusion, there is profound truth in the complete understanding of the two principles that govern Christian giving. There are also important consequences of this truth for the way we choose to give. Love is the foundation of true giving, giving that pleases God, and nothing else counts.

11

Freedom

I tell you the truth, everyone who sins is a slave
to sin. Now a slave has no permanent place in
the family, but a son belongs to it forever. So if
the Son sets you free, you will be free indeed.

—John 8:34–36

ALL ALONG, THE point of this book has been to convey one
message: we are free to give in a manner which pleases the
Spirit, not in a manner conforming to the written code of the
old covenant. Back in the beginning, I wrote that the purpose
of this book is to annihilate the notion that the tithe is still
(or was ever) binding on believers in Christ after his death. If
you have made it this far into the book, I cannot imagine that
you do not agree with me. There is simply no such thing as

a Christian tithe. If you still believe otherwise, my challenge to you is this: look up "tithe", "tenth", "money", "give", "pay", "owe", "debt", "riches", "wealth", "share", "contribution", "collection", and all the variations on these words, as well as any others you can think of, in an exhaustive concordance and make up your own mind. Do the research, check the facts, and I believe you will see that there is no way that the tithe still applies to Christians.

Jesus set us free from the yoke of the tithe. But not only are we now free to give, one of the great truths I discovered in writing this book is that we are absolutely free in every way! I never realized the important theme of freedom running throughout the New Testament. This is what makes Christianity *fundamentally different* than every other theistic religion. The freedom that Christ offers has been a stumbling block to some in that you cannot control the masses by preaching freedom. Guilt and shame are the most common devices that are used to manipulate people for the sake of religion, but God sought to change this.

> Therefore, there is now no condemnation for those who are in Christ Jesus, because through Christ Jesus the law of the Spirit of life has set me free from the law of sin and death. (Rom. 8:2)

Guilt and shame are frequently used in the message of the tithe. And I was once bound by this message. I was bound by what I knew to be true of the tithe (or should I say, what I did not know). But now that I know the truth of Scripture, I will never tithe again.

> If you hold to my teaching, you are really my disciples. Then you will know the truth, and the truth will set you free. (John 8:31–32)

His truth has set me free to give in a way that indeed pleases Him.

Consider the meaning of Galatians 5:1, "It is for freedom's sake that Christ has set you free" (Gal. 5:1).

I used to think this verse was redundant. Now I realize that it is not redundant, but it is remarkably profound. Christ could have set us free for many different reasons. Maybe God needed more priests in heaven, or soldiers in his army, and we were set free in order to serve. Or maybe God set us free to fulfill some other purpose. But the most wonderful truth is that he set us free because that is the way he intended us to live. He had no ulterior motives. He had no secret agenda. In His overwhelming love for us, he simply set us free, period. He paid the price for our freedom and does not expect anything in return. If this isn't true giving, I don't know what is.

Some people say, "You owe God *everything*. You owe God 100 percent. Be glad He only asks for 10 percent." Or they will say that it all *belongs* to God. I disagree, and I don't believe I'm being disrespectful to God. I don't *owe* God anything. You don't *owe* anything toward a *free gift. God's gift of life is free.* Christianity is, at its core, an acceptance of the free gift of eternal life in the form of Jesus Christ. If you accept this gift, all of your penalties for violations against God's Law are paid. If you reject this gift, you must try to pay for your violations.

Under the old covenant, people had to *pay* other people to mediate between themselves and God. The Israelites had to pay a group of people, the Levites and priests, to offer the penalty of their sin to God in the form of a sacrifice. They couldn't pay the penalty themselves. The penalty could only be paid (i.e., a sacrifice could only be made) by the priests. Israelites had to provide both the payment for their sins and the payment for the service of offering it. What financed the existence of people qualified to offer a sacrifice to God? The *tithe* (every third year).

In Christianity, Jesus is both the payment for sin as well as the mediator which offers the payment. Jesus is *free*. He offers himself freely. You either accept this, or you reject this. If you accept this, you release the right to repay God. You forfeit your autonomy to transact with God, and you become His slave. Slaves do not repay their masters. Maybe I should restate this point. In Christianity, you don't "deal" with God. There is no bartering for blessing. There is no bargaining for what you want. You lose the right to transact with Him as if you and He were equals. There are no Jacobs in Christianity. You don't get to wrestle Him for a blessing. God changed Jacob's name to Israel, which means "contends with God". In Christianity, there is no "contending" with God. Christians don't contend; they forfeit. Instead, God gives freely, and you give freely. If you believe God wants something back for His gift, then you are going to want something back for your gifts. You're going to want God to pay you back (i.e., bless you), and you're going to want other people to pay you back. This is unavoidable. Your actions and your thoughts and inclinations will be the natural by-product of how you view God. You cannot, in righteousness, strive to be something God is not. Don't you see that it is *pride* that causes a man to think he can even attempt to repay God.

What we do owe God is gratitude. Gratitude is the debt to be paid. Don't you see how perverted it is to say that you *owe* God *money*? In your gratitude, even if you attempt to repay God, you will find that you cannot. What do you have that He lacks? Nothing. But God does tell us how we can "repay" Him: by giving to others.

Think about it; this isn't so far-fetched. Suppose Bill Gates finances the college education of some poor kid. The kid feels indebted and at the conclusion of his education vows to repay his benefactor, Bill Gates. He tells Bill Gates, "Don't worry, I'll pay you back." Bill Gates doesn't know quite what to make of this. What's a few tens of thousands of dollars to Bill Gates? It's nothing. He doesn't miss the money. It's absolutely pointless to try to give it back to him. It terms of money, what he did for the kid meant so much to the kid, but so little to him. What Bill Gates gave was an opportunity for success, not the money that purchased the opportunity. The kid can neither repay the money nor the opportunity. Bill Gates has all the money he needs and more. Accordingly, he also does not need an opportunity to succeed. What he will demand, in the light of the kid's gratitude, is that the kid pays it forward.

Bill Gates would say this, "The money I gave you was a free gift. It wasn't a loan. It's free. Therefore, I don't expect it back, and I don't want it back. Your thanks is payment enough. If you want to do anything for me, then repay the kindness to someone else. Pay it forward. Make the world a better place. Touch the world in ways that I cannot. Reach people I cannot. If what I did was good in any way, then be like me. Model this behavior for the world to see. But whatever you do, don't try to repay me with money. You insult the very intention of the gift by trying to pay it back to me." I tell you this is how God is with us.

If I have accomplished my goal so far, I have helped you to see the theological truth that you are free to give. However, this alone may not bring you true freedom in the area of money. As a friend of mine told me, "By saying that Christians are free to give, you are also saying that they are free *not* to give." If all this book does is relieve the guilt you may be feeling by not tithing, then I have failed.

What I have come to realize is that our enemy does not want us free in any way. The sad truth is that the people in the wealthiest nation in the history of the world are slaves to money. I am talking about you and me. I am talking about Americans at the dawn of the new millennium. I believe that the thinking of many Christians has been shaped more by modern American culture than by the teachings of the church. This is borne out by the way we spend our money. We Americans have a peculiar way of spending our money even if we do tithe. In fact, it has been my experience that once the church has received what it thinks is its fair share, it doesn't really care how you spend the other 90 percent. There are individuals and ministries who teach Christians how to manage their finances, but overall, the church only teaches on money matters that affect the church, like tithing. The implicit understanding is that God will take care of the rest if you give the first 10 percent in the form of a tithe.

It is my opinion that the doctrine of the tithe is the church's response to our culture's extremely powerful messages concerning money and lifestyle. Basically, the church doesn't see much money coming in by preaching freedom. So the church has adopted the pernicious doctrine of the tithe. However, the modern culture is winning this war of ideas (or doctrines) in a big way. Despite the predominance of the doctrine of the tithe, according to the Barna Group (a Christian survey organization), very few Christians actually tithe.

> Tracking data show that tithing among all born again adults (i.e., evangelical and non-evangelical, combined) has stayed within a range of 6% to 14% throughout the past decade, varying by a few percentage points since 1999. ("Americans Donate Billions to Charity, but Giving to Churches Has Declined", article from www.barna.org)

The ideals and customs instilled by culture are keeping people from obeying the command coming from almost every pulpit in America. This is a problem whether you agree with me on tithing or not. It is obvious that there is a tremendous cultural force in America that seeks to enslave people to money. The root of the problem is, of course, sin. Greed and fear are what drive the money practices of people in this culture.

A book that has greatly affected me and has helped me see why so few people are free to give is *Rich Dad, Poor Dad* by Robert Kiyosaki. In this book, Kiyosaki says that just about everybody has a "price". He would say that most of us have a price because we are both fearful and greedy at the same time. We are, first of all, afraid of being in the position of not having money, or "enough" money. So we do all kinds of things to get money. Once we get money, the greed inside us starts telling us what we could do with all our money. And, like many devices of the enemy, greed suggests that what we have is not *enough*. This is when the pattern is set. The pattern is that of the making money and spending it, making money and spending it in order to support our American lifestyles. This cycle is also known as the "rat race".

The rat race is propagated by the unceasing and mind-numbing message of this culture to possess *more!* You can't have *more* without a measure of greed. And once you have *more*, you'll find that it isn't quite enough. We are constantly bombarded with messages in the form of commercials and other advertisements from people that want us to spend money. After twenty or so years of this cerebral assault, these messages become beliefs as rock solid as our belief in God. Our culture worships money, and even our Christian faith is permeated by the ideals of American culture. The culture promotes having *more*, but it is ultimately fear that drives this cycle.

Of course, those in the rat race are in a horrible cycle of destruction (if not literal financial ruin, then certainly moral decay). The ultimate irony is that no matter how much money or wealth you possess, there is no earthly antidote to fear. If a person is gripped with fear or attacked by a spirit of fear, it doesn't matter what you possess. If you are poor, fear will try to convince you cannot survive on what you have. If you are wealthy, fear will bring to your mind all the awful things that could happen if you lose your wealth (the stigma of being poor, the embarrassment of having wealth and squandering it, having to change your lifestyle, losing certain comforts, etc.) Probably the best anyone in the rat race could hope for is being, as Kiyosaki calls them, "high-priced slaves". And as it pertains to high-priced slaves, it has been my experience that our churches are full of them!

For people in this country at this point in history, wealth and want, riches and poverty are ultimately spiritual conditions. If you are truly free from the sins of greed and fear, you will be free to give and free to live your life in a way that pleases God. However, if you are a slave to greed and fear, there will never be enough. You will never have much to give, no matter how much money you make. You will always feel guilty for not giving more. If greed and fear are present when you have little money, it is likely that you will remain poor. And if even if you become "rich", your life will not manifest the generosity that is the fruit of a Christian life.

Sadly, the doctrine and practice of tithing do nothing to combat greed and fear. Even if you give 10 percent of your income in the form of a tithe, it is still possible to spend the remainder in a manner that it entirely fear-driven and greedy. And if we look closely at what is going on, it is easy to see how tithing promotes greed and the pursuit of earthly possessions. After all, the Bible promises abundant earthly blessings for tithers. So a truly horrific situation is possible even among those who tithe. They are slaves to the law of Moses (with all of its curses) with their first 10 percent, and they are slaves to their own greed and fear with the other 90 percent.

The solution to the money problems of American Christians is not the tithe. The solution is found in the life of Paul. Consider this important account from Paul himself concerning his lifestyle:

> I have learned the secret of being content in any and every situation, whether well fed or hungry, whether living in plenty or in want. I can do everything through him who gives me strength. (Phil. 4:12–13)

Unfortunately, many Christians in this country aren't able to say the same thing. It has been my experience that people say all the time that they simply have a hard time making ends meet, let alone giving money for Kingdom work. And yet these people seem to make room for new/nice things. These people are *slaves* to their possessions, and they don't even know it! They aren't *free* to give money to God! They are slaves to their lifestyles—bondservants to a culture that wages war on the things of God. They have not learned the lesson that Jesus gives *both the freedom and the strength* to give.

I don't care if you make $25,000 a year or $250,000, you can be generous in what you give for Kingdom work. *However, the freedom to give generously comes at the expense of your lifestyle.* This is perhaps the most important truth you will take from this book, practically speaking. Do you want freedom? Or do you want the highest standard of living your income affords? You can't have both.

There are many individuals and ministries out there, even secular ones, that are very good at teaching the basics of money and finances. It's really not my intention to teach on exactly how to make room for giving other than to point it out. You must make the choice that your freedom to give is more important than your lifestyle. This is an extremely difficult choice to make. And once you've made it, it's even harder to live out because this culture promotes lifestyle almost above everything else. Jesus said that if something causes you to sin, cut it off. If you recognize that watching TV is the source of an ideal for a lifestyle contrary to the will of God, cut it off! If you realize that you must maintain a certain standard of living to fit comfortably in certain social crowds, cut them off! If you realize that you permit yourself particular luxuries that ultimately affect how much you can give, cut them off!

You must become a new financial creature. You must have the courage to go against the flow of your friends, family, coworkers, neighbors, etc., when it comes to lifestyle. And oddly enough, in this culture, this is a shame to bear. Many people absolutely cannot stand to be thought less wealthy than they actually are. In fact, people will go to great lengths to be thought more wealthy than they actually are. Do not be like these people! Their God is money. Have the guts to drive a car far beneath what you could afford. Be willing to be perceived as poor. Be willing to be considered "cheap" (in the things of this world). This is very hard, but it is not impossible. This is sacrifice, and this is what it means to be a mature Christian. As the pastor said in the introduction of chapter 2, this is where the rubber meets the road in our walk with God. God knows the truth, and someday, when all things are reckoned, you will be rewarded for making room to allow yourself to give.

Conclusion

CLEARLY, THE TRUTH of freedom has implications in the area of giving. For those living in the fulfillment of Christ's love and in the fullness of the Spirit, there are no rules for giving. Giving the right amount to the right person at the right time becomes irrelevant. God Himself guides your giving because you are free to give. Listing just some of the commandments concerning giving in the New Testament:

1. Give to those who ask (Matt. 6:30)
2. Give freely (Matt. 10:8)
3. Give to the poor (Luke 12:33)
4. Give to those who can't repay (Luke 14:12–13)
5. Give to preachers of the Gospel (1 Cor. 9)
6. Give in love (1 Cor. 13:3)
7. Give your fair share (2 Cor. 8:13–15)
8. Give cheerfully (2 Cor. 9:7)

9. Give to teachers of the Bible (Gal. 6:6)
10. Give to your family (1 Tim. 5:3–8)—and don't forget…
11. Pay your taxes (Romans 13:8)

It becomes apparent why the tithe has become obsolete. The Spirit must guide your giving. Christianity is not about compiling lists of acceptable behaviors; it is about following the Spirit in the way of love. If you do this, you can chuck the list, because you will always be giving in a manner which pleases God.

The bottom line is: forget the tithe and just give!

I really do think that this is the answer that every one of us has known from the beginning. I believe the reason that many people have difficulty tithing is that a still, small voice says no. I believe that the Holy Spirit interferes with Christians who tithe, because He is always fighting for truth. And the truth is that God does not want you to give out of a sense of obligation. *He wants you to give as freely as He has given to you.*

As for giving in general, let us encourage deeds of charity that exercise our spiritual freedom. The real issue is the way in which we give. Let's give God's way. Let's be moved by the Spirit. Let's take what Jesus said at face value and be willing to obey at all costs. I'd like to see what happens then.

Finally...

Realize that you are free to give.

Recognize that giving to God takes on many forms.

Seek the counsel of the Holy Spirit.

Let Love be your guiding motivation.

And be prepared to do something even harder than tithing.